TITANIC
DESTINATION DISASTER
The Legends and the Reality

An expert summary of the world's
most famous maritime tragedy

TITANIC
DESTINATION DISASTER

The Legends and the Reality

John P. Eaton &
Charles A. Haas

W · W · NORTON & COMPANY
NEW YORK · LONDON

First American Edition 1987

W. W. Norton & Company Inc.,
500 Fifth Avenue, New York, N.Y.10110.
W. W. Norton & Company Ltd.,
37 Great Russell Street, London WC1B 3NU.

Printed and bound in Great Britain.

ISBN 0-393-30492-2

1 2 3 4 5 6 7 8 9 0

Cover illustrations *Chris Mayger's famous depiction (front) uses a certain degree of artist's licence but nevertheless captures movingly the atmosphere of the disaster scene. Michael V. Ralph's painting (back) shows lifeboats five and seven, carrying just a fraction of their capacity, leaving the doomed* Titanic *as another distress rocket vainly sears the night sky.*

Contents

Introduction

TITANIC
The very name conjures up thoughts of disaster and doom, of inevitable fate, of man's fallibility.

TITANIC. . .

The world's newest and most beautiful passenger liner, whose maiden voyage from the Old World to the New was cut short by collision with an iceberg, resulting in a loss of 1,523 lives.

Titanic. If the ship had not been lost in one of maritime history's most memorable disasters, her name would probably still have lived today, but for rather different reasons. The luxury and comfort of her passenger accommodation exceeded those of any vessel of her day. Her size was greater than any other ship. Her equipment and engines, the integrity of her construction, were the best that money could buy.

If *Titanic* had been allowed to live out her normal, expected life span, she would have taken her rightful place in the pantheon of great liners: *Mauretania, Aquitania, Europa, Queen Mary, Normandie, United States*. . . Ships of luxury and comfort, ships of beauty.

In her brief life *Titanic* was a ship of pride and bright honour to her owners and builders, and to the countries which claimed her as their own.

During her single, interrupted voyage one element of misjudgement was added to another in a deadly chain. Warnings went unheeded. Errors in safety standards and navigation were combined and compounded to generate the inevitable tragic conclusion.

And from the ashes of her loss arose new rules for safety, for navigation, for judging ships themselves, and the men who sailed in them.

Titanic. . . As she lived, myth and legend had already begun to form around her. Her passengers and her crew for the voyage were the stuff of which legends are made. Even the facts of her loss assumed an air of fantasy. And when the fertile imaginations of contemporary journalists and writers began to stir the mixture of fantasy and fact, myth and legend into a single swirling tale of tragedy, an aura was created which, today, makes it difficult to separate fiction from fact; indeed it makes it difficult to discover and authenticate fact itself.

When considering *Titanic*'s facts, myth and fantasy must also be given due regard. Seldom has there been an ocean liner about which so many facts are known. Never has there been a ship whose history is clouded by so many fallacies, whose very legend seems to endure because of these fabled traditions.

Titanic's life begins on 31 March 1909 when her keel was laid down. It continues through her launch on 31 May 1911 and her triumphant 10 April 1912 departure on her maiden voyage. It ends in the early hours of 15 April 1912 when her stern plates vanished beneath the chill, starlit North Atlantic waters.

But her name lives on in the imagination, captured by the elusive blend of romance and realism.

Titanic's life, her loss, her legend weave a fabric of wonder and disbelief. From beginning to end they tell of a beautiful liner's incredible voyage through history's pages, and of her ultimate fate, her. . .

Destination Disaster.

ONE

'Iceberg, Right Ahead!'

Aboard *Titanic*. At sea. Westbound.

Sunday, 14 April, 1912.

Ashore it was another day of rest, at sea a day of routine activity. There were meals to be prepared and served, brightwork to be polished, decks to be scraped and sanded, passengers to be tended to. On this maiden voyage there was equipment to be checked, performances to be monitored and recorded. And far below there were boilers to be fired, coal passed and trimmed, steam pressure to be maintained, all to speed the ship westwards.

In the saloons and smoking rooms there were rumours of a record crossing. Many passengers and, indeed, some crew believed the company wished to display its new liner in a most favourable light by bringing her across to New York with a new speed record. The rumours had some basis. Each day at sea, from noon to noon, had seen an increasing number of miles logged. There was talk that the White Star Line's managing director J. Bruce Ismay had called chief engineer Joseph Bell to his cabin while *Titanic* was stopped at Queenstown. There the two men purportedly had discussed the feasibility of setting a speed record during the crossing.

Indeed, there had been a discussion between the men. But it was concerned mainly with the amount of coal in the bunkers (a logical point, in view of the recent coal strike), and of *not* driving the ship too fast lest she arrive at New York late on Tuesday night (instead of on Wednesday morning, as planned) and be unable to enter the harbour and dock safely.

Ismay later testified at the British inquiry that he had talked with Bell about the possibility of driving the vessel at full speed for several hours on Monday if the weather were suitable. *Titanic* never had been truly tested at full draught, top-speed conditions, and such an all-out but brief run would give builders' representatives and the ship's own engineering staff a chance to collect additional data.

Sunday saw 24 of *Titanic*'s 29 boilers in service. During the day preparations were made to light the remaining boilers to make ready for the next day's speed test. But the boilers were never actually lit. Even with approximately 84 per cent of her boilers operating, *Titanic*'s engines drove the propellers at 75 revolutions per minute, giving a speed of 21½ knots, almost 24½ land miles per hour. Top speed was estimated to be over 22 knots, perhaps as high as 24. Whatever the figure, it would surely be nowhere near the *Mauretania*'s 26-knot record. Monday's high speed run might tell. . .

Sunday saw two breaks in shipboard routine: there was no daily inspection of the vessel, and Divine Service was held. At 10.30 am passengers from all classes convened in the first class dining saloon. Led by Captain Smith, the service was not from the Church of England's Book of Common Prayer but, rather, from the company's own prayer book. The ship's orchestra provided music for the service which concluded shortly after 11 am with the fine old hymn, 'O God Our Help in Ages Past'.

Even as he led Divine Service Captain Smith was aware that a potential danger loomed — quite literally — over the horizon. At 9 am, ship's time, *Titanic* had received a wireless message from *Caronia*, eastbound from New York to Liverpool via Queenstown.

> Captain, *Titanic* — West-bound steamers report bergs, growlers and field ice in 42 degrees North from 49 degrees to 51 degrees West, April 12. Compliments, Barr.

The message was delivered to Captain Smith on the bridge. After noting it he posted it for his officers to read.

Sunday, 14 April. The day was bright and clear. During the afternoon it became noticeably cool. Passengers deserted the decks and sought comfort and warmth in the spacious lounge, the cozy library or the comfortable smoking room. The murmur of conversation was punctuated by an occasional genteel laugh, the rattle of tea cups, the clink of glasses. The veranda café's outer doors were slid closed. But seated in the red and brown cushioned wicker furniture there, young merrymakers could still watch the sea speed past through the bronze-framed windows nearly seven feet tall.

In the first class reading room — its floor carpeted in old rose, its windows hung with pink draperies — passengers leisurely read books and the latest magazines placed there by the *Times* of London's book club.

The library's quiet contrasted with the convivial atmosphere of the smoking room where whist, bridge and poker games were in full swing. Here there was no sea view: light entered through painted glass windows depicting landscapes, ancient ships and historic and mythological figures. Over the marble fireplace hung a large oil painting, 'Plymouth Harbour', by the well-known British painter Norman Wilkinson. (Wilkinson had also painted the picture that hung above *Olympic*'s fireplace, 'Approach to the New World', which depicted a New York Harbour view.)

In the main lounge a trio from the ship's orchestra played the day's popular songs: music from operetta, the musical stage, or the new sensation, ragtime; salon pieces, reminiscent of a smart continental café; selections from 'The Quaker Girl', 'The Chocolate Soldier', and 'The Merry Widow'. Gems from Gilbert and Sullivan operettas 'Mikado', 'Pirates of Penzance', 'Iolanthe'; waltzes by Strauss and Waldteufel; the popular waltz 'Songe d'Automne' by the British composer Joyce; 'Oh, You Beautiful Doll', 'Alexander's Ragtime Band', 'The Navajo Rag'. . .

The second class smoking room aft on B deck, and the second class library, directly below on C deck, were no less thronged with conversing passengers, while others, such as Mrs Esther Hart, rested in their cabins. But most strolled the corridors. Children played in the enclosed promenades flanking the library. The brown carpet and mahogany, tapestry-covered furniture in the second class library were well set off by the green silk draperies, creating a comfort and intimacy usually found on other liners only in first class accommodation. It was a splendid apartment in which to spend a cold, bright April afternoon at sea.

The falling temperatures also drove indoors the men, women and children of third class. Unlike most Atlantic liners, *Titanic* contained public rooms for them, as well. While scarcely luxurious, these were comfortable and clean. This Sunday afternoon, with the after and forward well deck promenades chilled by falling temperatures, the public rooms' warmth and companionship were especially welcome.

For the men there was the smoking room and two bars — one forward in the open space on D deck and another adjacent to the smoking room at C deck's after end. Women and children had the general room, to starboard of the smoking room. And it may be assumed that, with or without stewards' approval, children used the lower decks' stairs and corridors for their games.

There were no games, no relaxation for the ship's two wireless operators: John George Phillips, senior Marconi operator, age 24, wage £4 5s (£4.25) a month; Harold Sidney Bride, junior Marconi operator, age 22, wage £2 2s 6d (£2.12½, or less than $12) a month. Though signed on with the crew (their official title, 'telegraphist') the two men were actually employees of the Marconi International Marine Communication Company, Ltd.

Under its agreement with the Marconi Company, the White Star Line was provided with free wireless messages between the ship, its owners or other ships regarding navigation, safety, or ship's business, provided the messages did not exceed a 30-words-per-day average. Excess wordage was charged to the ship's owners at half the current tariff rate. In return, White Star was to provide the Marconi operators with their meals and lodging.

On this Sunday, 14 April, Bride and Phillips had been busy receiving, logging and transmitting passenger messages. Wireless transmitting and receiving ranges increased markedly at night, and night signals from the powerful British land station at Poldhu (call letters MPD) relayed by intermediate ships had included news, stock reports and some personal messages.

The news bulletins were typed by the purser and posted in the first class smoking room. (It was not for another six weeks — commencing 1 June 1912 — that these 'bulletins' were formalized into a printed sheet, the *Ocean Times*, for distribution among White Star passengers.)

There also had been the day traffic: personal messages to and from *Titanic*'s passengers. The ship's 1½ kilowatt wireless apparatus, among the most powerful afloat, had a 400-mile daytime transmitting range. This trebled at night, but during the day, particularly now in mid-Atlantic, its function was limited to 'conversations' with other ships.

Signals were transmitted and received on closely-adjacent standard frequencies, with two, three or even more signals being sent or received at the same time. Much of the operator's skill involved being able to discriminate and select the particular message addressed to his station. To assist operators, each station had its particular identifying call letters. With few exceptions, call letters for British ships generally began with 'M', while those of German ships started with 'D' and United States naval vessels with 'N'. *Titanic*'s were MGY, while her sister *Olympic* had MKC.

The hours were long, the work tedious and pressure-filled. At least Bride and Phillips were fortunate to be working together, so they might set shifts and 'spell' one another at the key. In 1912 laws did not require two operators or 24-hour manning of ships' wireless. Many passenger liners and all freighters had single operators whose long, tiring hours were unrelieved except for brief naps.

Operators were supposed to intercept for their own captain's attention all messages relating to navigation and safety of his vessel. Thus on this Sunday, 14 April, *Titanic*'s operators received several messages regarding ice conditions in an area for which *Titanic* was now headed directly. At 9 am a message from *Caronia* was taken immediately to the bridge, where it was posted for the officers' attention. *Titanic*'s position at this time was 43.35 N 43.50 W, and her course S 62° W. Her position had changed to 42.34 N, 45.50 W by 1.42 pm, when a message was received from *Athinai* via *Baltic*:

> Capt Smith, *Titanic*:
> . . .Greek steamer *Athinai* reports passing icebergs and large quantities of field
> ice today in latitude 41.51 N, longitude 49.52 W.

This message placed icebergs within a few miles of *Titanic*'s track. It, too, was taken immediately to the bridge and very shortly thereafter to Captain Smith, who was lunching with J. Bruce Ismay. The captain handed the message to Ismay with the remark that the ship soon might be encountering ice. Ismay put the message in his pocket and later showed it to several passengers, repeating Smith's statement. The message was not posted on the bridge nor entered in the scrap log until 7.15 pm when Captain Smith requested its return from Ismay.

At 5.50 pm, slightly ahead of schedule, *Titanic* reached the 'Corner', the position along the 42nd degree of north latitude at which, according to sailing orders, the ship was to cross the 47th degree of west longitude. At this point the course was changed from S 62° W to S 86° W.

As the bright day turned to dusk and then to dark, the cool air began to turn cold. As passengers prepared for and ate dinner in the dining saloons' warm comfort, the outside temperature was dropping. At 7 pm it was 43 degrees. Because of the day's wireless messages, an iceberg watch was ordered. At 7.15 pm the officer of the watch, first officer William Murdoch, ordered lamp trimmer Samuel Hemming to secure the forward fo'c's'le hatch to prevent glow from interfering with the crow's nest watch.

By 7.30 pm, a mere half-hour later, the temperature had dropped five degrees, to 39 degrees. At this time, as fourth officer Joseph Boxhall, responsible for navigation, took a star sighting, a message from the freighter *Californian* to the eastbound freighter *Antillian* was overheard by *Titanic*'s wireless operator. Harold Bride delivered the message to the bridge and handed it to an officer. (Later, Bride could not recall whom.) The message reported ice at 42.3 N 49.9 W about 19 miles north of *Titanic*'s track. This message was not taken to Captain Smith personally, as he was in the *à la carte* restaurant attending a party given by Mr and Mrs George D. Widener. Other guests included the Carters, the Thayers, and presidential aide Major Archibald Butt.

The ship sped on, the time passed: 8 pm. . . 8.30 pm. . . At 8.40 pm second officer Lightoller, now officer of the watch, ordered ship's carpenter J. Maxwell to watch the fresh water supply as it might freeze. 9 pm. . . The air temperature had fallen to 33 degrees.

At about 8.50 pm Captain Smith bade his dinner companions 'good night' and made his way to the bridge. Upon his arrival Lightoller briefed him about weather conditions and the ice precautions that had already been taken. Remarking that the night was quite clear, the captain left the bridge at about 9.30, telling Lightoller that if visibility or weather conditions 'become at all doubtful, let me know at once. I will be just inside'. He then went to his cabin on the starboard side behind the bridge.

9.40 pm. . . In the wireless 'shack' Bride had turned in for a nap before working the busy late night traffic. Phillips was manning the apparatus alone when a message was received from the westbound *Mesaba*:

> To *Titanic* and eastbound ships:
> Ice report in latitude 42 N, to 41.25 N, longitude 49 W, to 50.30 W. Saw much heavy pack ice and great number large icebergs. Also field ice. Weather good, clear.

The land station at Cape Race, Newfoundland (call letters MCE) was in range now, and Phillips was very busy transmitting messages which had accumulated during the day. Unable or unwilling to leave his set unattended, he 'spiked' the *Mesaba*'s ice message.

During the two hours and forty minutes of Titanic*'s sinking, the wireless station at Cape Race (MCE) relayed disaster news to ships at sea and, over land telephone lines, to Montreal, Quebec for distribution to the rest of North America. (*Canadian Marconi Company.*)*

(Later, perhaps, when relieved by Bride, he might have a chance to take it down the corridor to the bridge. . . Later, perhaps. . .) The message, which described ice directly ahead of *Titanic*, never did get to the bridge.

10 pm. . . Four bells. . . First officer Murdoch relieved second officer Lightoller on the bridge. Look-outs Reginald Lee and Frederick Fleet climbed the iron ladder inside the forward mast to the look-out's cage, where they relieved Archie Jewell and George Symons. Before they departed, Symons passed the word received earlier from Lightoller to keep a careful look-out for bergs and growlers.

Lights gleaming, *Titanic* sped through the night at 21 knots. The sea was calm, perfectly flat. There was no moon, though the stars shone brilliantly. There was indeed a chill in the air. Between 7 pm and 10 pm the air temperature had dropped from 43 to 32 degrees.

The minutes passed.

At about 10.30 pm a steamer was sighted on an opposite course. It was the Furness-Withy freighter *Rappahannock*. Her acting master Albert E. Smith signalled the nearby liner with his morse lamp. 'Have just passed through heavy field ice and several icebergs'. After a brief pause *Titanic* replied, also by signal light, 'Message received. Thanks. Good night'.

Rappahannock vanished eastwards. *Titanic* continued on her course, speed undiminished.

In the wireless quarters, Phillips was still busily engaged in the Cape Race traffic and in sending and receiving messages to and from other ships. A few minutes before 11 pm his concentration was abruptly interrupted by a signal from a nearby ship, a signal so loud that it probably deafened him momentarily. It was from the freighter *Californian*, twenty or so miles away to the north: 'We are stopped and surrounded by ice'. Still smarting from the loud intrusion, his own signals jammed, Phillips interrupted: 'Shut up. I am busy. I am working Cape Race'.

Californian's wireless operator, Cyril Furmstone Evans, tired from his long, lonely day with the wireless apparatus and now rebuffed, listened for several more minutes to *Titanic*'s

Cape Race traffic. Then, around 11.30 pm, he turned off his equipment, took off his earphones and turned in. In his fatigued state he didn't bother to rewind his mechanically powered detector. It had been a long day. . .the rewinding could wait until morning.

11.30 pm. . . Seven bells. . . Less than five miles ahead *Titanic*'s destiny awaited. . .

Fred Fleet and Reginald Lee swung their arms and tried to keep warm in the frigid blasts caused by the ship's rapid forward motion. In the look-out cage's narrow confines fifty feet above the fo'c's'le deck this was not easy to do. The air was cold and they still had more than twenty minutes before their midnight relief. Their eyes strained to pierce the night's darkness ahead and around them. Moments before, what seemed to be a slight mist or haze had appeared on the horizon and a moist, clammy smell filled the air. The men wished they had something to aid their vision. (When *Titanic* left Belfast there had been binoculars in the look-out's cage. But very shortly after departure from Southampton, before the ship reached Queenstown, it was discovered that the binoculars had been removed. None of the officers seemed to know why or by whose orders.)

Suddenly, without a word to Lee, Fleet hunched forward and peered intently ahead. His hand reached for the lanyard of the sixteen-inch brass bell which hung several feet above the crow's nest. Still staring forward Fleet gave the cord three sharp pulls. The bell's brittle sound fractured the night's stillness. Fleet then reached across to the telephone in its compartment on the starboard side and urgently rang its bell.

After a short interval — it must have seemed long minutes to Fleet — sixth officer James P. Moody answered on the bridge. Fleet's message was brief, Moody's response even more so:

'Iceberg right ahead.'

'Thank you.'

Fleet and Lee gripped the crow's nest rail. They could see the huge berg's irregular, pinnacled shape, a black hulk against the night's darkness, blotting out increasing numbers of stars as it came nearer and nearer to the speeding liner's starboard bow.

Left *The Leyland Line steamer*
California. (Harper's.)

Right *A sketch of the iceberg was prepared later under the direction of Joseph Scarrott,* Titanic *seaman.* (Daily Graphic.)

On the bridge first officer Murdoch acted almost immediately on Moody's repeat of the message, using the instincts of a good officer with more than twenty years at sea. He gave the order 'Hard-a-starboard' and at the same time telegraphed to the engine room 'Stop. Full speed astern'. In almost the same movement he pulled the lever, electrically closing the fifteen watertight doors in the engine and boiler room bulkheads.

The telemotor wheel spun by quartermaster Robert Hichens inside the enclosed wheelhouse did its job well. *Titanic* had turned two points (22½ degrees) to port before the collision occurred. (Later experiments with *Titanic*'s almost-identical sister *Olympic* showed that at 21½ knots it would take about 37 seconds to produce a course change of two points once the wheel was hard over. In this time the ship would travel about 466 yards.)

At the start of her port turn, *Titanic*'s bow began to swing away from the approaching berg. To Fleet and Lee it seemed as though a collision might have been avoided. The berg's dark mass was level with *Titanic*'s bow, then slipped past along the starboard side, its top more than 25 feet above the crow's nest platform.

Though there was no apparent collision with the berg, large ice chunks fell from it, cascading onto the forward well deck as though dislodged by some vibration deep within the berg.

The berg's dark bulk glided along the ship's length, scraping and bumping against the first 300 feet of the vessel's hull deep below the waterline. As *Titanic* was still moving at about 21 knots she would have passed through 300 feet in less than ten seconds. The ice passed amidships and Murdoch ordered the helm hard to port so that the stern would clear. As the berg receded beyond the stern, the look-outs for the first time saw a tip of white at the iceberg's very crest, which appeared to be emitting an almost-luminous haze.

Bobbing slightly from the impact, the berg disappeared from view, astern.

Many passengers and crew were only slightly disturbed by the collision. Some who slept were not even awakened. To seaman W. Brice on watch outside the seamen's mess, it felt like a heavy vibration, not a violent shock or bad jar. It was a rumbling noise that continued for about ten seconds. Other crew members thought the ship had lost a propeller or that the engines had suddenly been placed full astern. Several described it as a scraping or grinding sound on the ship's bottom, as though the anchor had suddenly been let go and its chain was dragging along the side.

Passengers' descriptions were more vivid. Preparing for bed in cabin A20 Lady Lucile Duff-Gordon described it 'as though someone had drawn a giant finger all along the side of the boat'. Mrs J. Stuart White, in cabin C32, said, 'It did not seem to me there was any great impact at all. It was as though we went over about a thousand marbles'.

Second class passenger Lawrence Beesley in cabin D56 recalled, 'There was nothing more than what seemed to be an extra heave of the engines and a more than usually obvious dancing of the mattress on which I sat. Nothing more than that — no sound of a crash or of anything else; no sense of shock, no jar that felt like one heavy body meeting another'.

Look-out Reginald Lee, who had observed the actual collision, noted, 'She heeled slightly

Above left *First class passenger Archibald Gracie knew there was something amiss when, following the collision, the ship stopped and began to blow off steam.* (The Truth About the Titanic.)

Above right *Science teacher Lawrence Beesley felt the shock of the berg's impact in his second class cabin, D56. He said it was 'a more than usually obvious dancing of the mattress on which I sat'.* (Illustrated London News.)

to port as she struck along the starboard side. There was the sound of rending metal right away; it seemed to be running right along the starboard side'.

Deep inside the ship, in number six boiler room, on the starboard side, forward, leading stoker Frederick Barrett heard the impact's crunching and then a sound like thunder rolling forward towards him. Before his startled eyes suddenly appeared a line of water pouring through a thin gash in the ship's side about two feet above the stokehold floor. Barrett barely escaped up the boiler room's emergency ladder. The watertight doors slid closed amid the raucous shrilling of the alarm bells activated by Murdoch on the bridge.

Roused from his rest by the collision, Captain Smith rushed up on to the bridge. 'What have we struck, Mr Murdoch?'

'An iceberg sir. I hard-a-starboarded and reversed the engines and I was going to hard-a-port around it, but she was too close. I could not do any more'.

'Have you closed the watertight doors?' demanded the master.

'They are already closed, sir'.

Smith and Murdoch hurried to the starboard bridge wing and peered aft into the darkness looking for the berg.

Returning inside, the commander ordered fourth officer Boxhall, who had just arrived on the bridge, to inspect the forward area below and report back to him as quickly as possible.

The other officers, alerted by Boxhall, hurriedly presented themselves on the bridge. Boxhall returned about fifteen minutes later to report that while he had seen no damage above F deck, a postal clerk had told him water was entering the sorting room on G deck and the mail was being moved.

A rock-hard protrusion from the iceberg had struck *Titanic*'s hull about fifteen feet above the keel and had then sliced along the steel plates, opening up a narrow, intermittent gash which penetrated the forepeak tank, numbers 1, 2 and 3 holds, and the forward boiler room (number 6). It was later demonstrated that the total area opened to the sea by the impact did not exceed twelve square feet.

But the 'twelve square feet' extended over 300 feet of the ship's length and allowed five compartments to flood. *Titanic* could float with any two of her watertight compartments flooded. She could float with even the first four compartments breached. But she could not float with water filling the first five compartments.

Only number one bulkhead, the first one forward, extended to the uppermost continuous deck, C. Bulkheads two and eleven to fifteen extended to the second continuous deck, D, while bulkheads three to nine extended only to the third continuous deck, E. The forward bulkheads would have contained water in the first four compartments so it would not have risen above D deck. But flooding of the fifth compartment — boiler room number six — caused water to rise above E deck, thus spilling over into the sixth compartment and causing the bow to be pulled further under. This in turn permitted water to flow into successive compartments, each pulling the bow still further down until the ship foundered.

From the moment that thin jet of water spurted through the plating in front of Barrett's startled eyes, *Titanic* was doomed.

There were those who said *Titanic* had been doomed from the start, from the moment the hull number 390904 had been assigned by her builders — a number some Harland and Wolff yard workers read in mirror images as 'NO POPE.'

If this were not enough to cause fear and doubt in the minds of the superstitious, a horoscope cast for a 31 May 1911 birth (*Titanic*'s launch date) at 12.15 pm on latitude 54°36′N, longitude 5°56′W, (the co-ordinates of Belfast) predicted, among other things, danger on or near water, accidents in travel and sorrow and loss through relatives.

Superstitions notwithstanding, many factors contributed to *Titanic*'s loss. Some of them — design and outfitting flaws — were correctable; some — faulty navigation, failure to deliver warning messages — were the result of human errors; some — collision and near-collision, weather conditions — were unpredictable. Yet all occurred in their proper sequence, in their proper place and time, and combined to provide an unalterable schedule for disaster.

If the design of the *Titanic* herself had called for watertight bulkheads to be carried one deck higher there would have been no overflow, no spillage from forward to after compartments, pulling the ship's head lower in the water and causing further overflow. If the Board of Trade's lifeboat capacity requirements had been more up to date (the last major rules revision was in 1894 when few ships exceeded 10,000 tons), and had demanded boat capacity for all persons on board, there would not have been so many crew and passengers lost.

By 18 September 1911 *Titanic*'s maiden voyage date had been set: 20 March 1912. What if *Olympic* had not collided with the cruiser *Hawke* at Southampton on 20 September? Following this accident, *Olympic* had to return to Belfast for repairs, usurping the large dry-dock, equipment and workers which might otherwise have been used for *Titanic*'s construction. *Olympic*'s presence at Belfast delayed *Titanic*'s completion and caused her owners to set 10 April as the date for the new liner's first departure. Would *Titanic*'s accident have occurred if there had not been the three-week postponement?

On sailing day. . . What if *Titanic* had actually collided with *New York* while departing from her pier? What if the pilot's and the commander's skills had not been sufficient to avoid an accident? A collision, no matter how slight, would have delayed the voyage for how long? Hours? Days?

What of the time *Titanic*'s departure was delayed by the near-collision in Southampton? What of the hour or more that was never actually made up?

For almost her entire voyage *Titanic* had been advised repeatedly of ice conditions at or near the position her sailing orders required her to occupy. Throughout the day of 14 April, as she approached this location, her wireless operators received at least six messages which described field ice and ice bergs on her course and directly ahead.

One message (from *Athinai* via *Baltic*) was not posted on the bridge until more than five hours after it had been received. Another message (at 7.30 pm, *Californian* to *Antillian*) was not shown to the captain, since to do so would have interrupted his dinner. Yet another message (from *Mesaba*) was never taken to the bridge as the wireless operator was working alone and could not leave his equipment. The receipt of a final, perhaps crucial message (from *Californian*) was interrupted and never completed when *Titanic*'s operator impatiently cut it off so that he might continue his own commercial traffic.

There had even been a visual warning at 10.30 pm from the *Rappahannock*, whose morse lamp message about the heavy field ice directly ahead was briefly acknowledged from *Titanic*'s bridge. There is no evidence that this vital information was ever heeded; nor was it given to Captain Smith, now dozing in his quarters.

The air was clear, the sea calm. There were no waves and there was no breeze. Either would have created a wash of water against the berg's base, giving it a low white 'collar' which would have stood out starkly against the dark water. The sky was moonless. On such a clear night, the light from even a quarter moon would have made the berg visible.

Recently — probably only an hour or two earlier — the iceberg had turned over in the sea. With its water-filled portion now above the surface, it thus presented a dark face, making it practically invisible against the night sky. An hour or two later the berg's face would have been lighter, perhaps even white as the water drained away, and visible. . .

The impact. . . Would it have been different if the look-out had spotted the berg sooner? (Perhaps the ship might have had time to dodge the ice?) Later? (Fewer watertight compartments would have been breached had the ship struck head-on. Ignobly down at the head but still afloat she might have been able to reach Halifax, 750 miles due west.)

Titanic's lifespan can be measured in hours, her maiden voyage in minutes. A slight shift of time — several minutes more, or several minutes less — would have changed the ship's position and put her ahead of or behind the precise spot where the berg was struck.

But once the flow of time began, there could be no modification. The inevitable was already set in motion. *Titanic* had but one destination: the disaster which was her doom.

After returning from his inspection trip Boxhall was ordered by Captain Smith to calculate *Titanic*'s position. Using the ship's course (since 5.50 pm South 86 West true), the 7.30 pm stellar observation he had taken, and his own *estimate* of the ship's speed as being 22 knots, Boxhall worked out a position based on dead reckoning.

(If he did not take into account the one-knot southerly current through which *Titanic* was passing, an error of as much as four miles in latitude could have entered his calculations. During the eight-to-midnight watch the ship's clocks were set back 23 minutes to compensate for westward progress. Did he remember this time change in gauging the distance travelled? And the ship's speed was 21½ knots, not the 22 he estimated. These elements, combined into a very rough estimate, might approximate an actual position four miles south and six miles east of the calculated position.)

Boxhall scribbled his calculation on a scrap of paper and promptly handed it to Captain Smith. The commander hastily strode to the wireless room, gave the paper to wireless operator Phillips and ordered a call for assistance.

'CQD. . . CQD. . . (It was the call to alert all stations within range; 'Come Quick, Danger,' some called it.) This was indeed a call for help, a plea for the safety of more than 2,200 lives. By 12.15 am the message was crackling through a cable piercing the Marconi room's roof on its way to the huge antenna that stretched between the masts, and sent hurtling through the night. 'CQD. . . CQD. . .' followed by *Titanic*'s position.

The signals were heard almost simultaneously by *La Provence*, *Mount Temple* and the land station at Cape Race. Interference from distance or other transmissions caused *Mount Temple* to hear the position as '41°46', 50°24' W', while Cape Race heard '41°44' N, 50°24' W'. At 12.18 am the ship *Ypiranga* also recorded the latter position in her wireless log.

But by 12.15 am the position was corrected to that which Boxhall had worked out:

> Come at once. We have struck a berg. It's a CQD, OM [old man]. Position 41°46' N, 50°14' W.

The ship to which this message was addressed. . . *Carpathia*.

Carpathia's sole wireless operator, 21-year-old Harold Thomas Cottam, had been on duty since 7 am Sunday 14 April. He was tired and wished to go to bed. There was, however, one last message he waited to receive, a confirmation of an earlier transmission he'd sent to the Allan liner *Parisian*. Except for this he would have shut down his station half an hour earlier and gone to bed.

Still there was no message. Half-undressed, Cottam idly switched his receiver to the frequency used for ships nearby, hoping to kill a few moments in communication with *Titanic*. About an hour earlier, while waiting for *Parisian*'s message, he had been listening to the land station at Cape Cod. This station had many messages for *Titanic* but could not interrupt the White Star ship's exchanges with Cape Race.

Finding *Titanic*'s frequency and hearing a momentary lull, Cottam broke in with:

'I say, old man, do you know there is a batch of messages coming through for you from MCC [Cape Cod]?'

Scarcely waiting for completion of Cottam's message, Phillips responded with the distress transmission. Cottam could not believe his ears. 'Shall I tell my captain? Do you require assistance?'

From MGY [*Titanic*]: 'Yes. Come quick!'

Cottam tore off his headphones and ran forward to the bridge. He burst in and blurted out the distress message to the officer of the watch, first officer H. V. Dean, who did not wait for a repetition. With Cottam propelled in front, the two men quickly descended the steep steps to the captain's cabin.

Captain Arthur Rostron had just gone to bed. Dean and Cottam pushed their way into his cabin without knocking and, rightfully, the master was irritated. Upon hearing the message he paused only to confirm it with Cottam. Then, hurriedly pulling on his uniform, he ascended to the bridge and consulted the navigation chart.

Rostron soon established that the Mediterranean-bound *Carpathia* was about 58 miles south-east of *Titanic*'s distress position, and that the most direct course to her was North 52 degrees West. *Carpathia* wheeled around to head north-west on her new course. Alerted by the bridge, the engine room officers and crew began building pressure in *Carpathia*'s ten-year-old boilers. The off-duty watches of the 'black gang' were called to add their efforts in the stokeholds. Before the night was over, the ship would comfortably exceed her registered 14½ knot top speed, achieving over 17 knots.

As *Carpathia* surged forward, Rostron assembled his officers and issued a series of orders to prepare the ship and her crew for receiving survivors. One of the many heroic acts performed that night, Rostron's commands were textbook examples of preparation and foresight. Issued under the great pressure of the moment, they demonstrated superbly the master's knowledge and skill. Cabins and public rooms were to be readied to accommodate survivors. Hot coffee and food were to be prepared, nets and portable lights strung along the ship's sides, gangways to be readied, slings rigged, canvas bags put in place to haul up the children, oil to be poured down the forward lavatories to make the surface of the sea outside as smooth as possible.

But for *Titanic,* the object of *Carpathia*'s mission, the drama had already taken an unlikely, unpredictable turn. . .

After the collision but before completely stopping *Titanic* briefly moved ahead at half speed under Captain Smith's orders. Evidence from a crewman on the fo'c's'le indicates that the ship's wheel must have been ordered hard-a-port immediately after impact, to prevent *Titanic*'s stern from striking the iceberg. Therefore, as she slowed to a halt in the calm water *Titanic* described a great arc to starboard. Once stopped, she drifted in the one knot southerly current.

In the twenty minutes following the collision Captain Smith received damage reports. He consulted with the ship's designer, Thomas Andrews, and was advised that his command — the newest, largest, safest ship afloat — had but little more than two hours to live.

At midnight it became 15 April. Even with the ship stopped, most crew routines proceeded normally. The engine room relief watch, though not yet ordered below to their posts, stood by. In the crow's nest Lee and Fleet were relieved by Hogg and Evans. (It is unlikely that the order to 'Keep a sharp watch for ice' was passed along.) Stewards put finishing touches to the dining rooms' breakfast table settings.

But on deck — amid the roar and hiss of now-unnecessary steam exhausting overhead — the new day's first order was an unusual one: 'Muster the crew. Stand by to uncover boats'.

Titanic's deck crew had never acted as one to man and lower the ship's boats. A departure day test lowering for the Board of Trade inspector at Southampton had involved just two boats and their respective crews. Now, untrained and untried (perhaps some actually unfamiliar with the relatively new Welin davits), the deck crew turned out and hastened to the boat deck.

Chief officer Wilde assigned second officer Lightoller to see to the stripping of the boats' covers. Running forward to boat 4 on the port side, Lightoller began pulling off the cover himself. As two or three men arrived, they were put to work at the task and Lightoller then directed the deck hands coming on deck to other boats on port and starboard sides. He used hand signals; the din of escaping steam made verbal commands impossible.

After making a complete circuit of the boat deck, parcelling out crewmen as he went, Lightoller asked Wilde if the boats should be swung out. Lightoller later said he believed Wilde had said 'No', or 'Wait'. Moments later, Captain Smith did give the order from the bridge to swing out the boats.

The tale of port side lifeboat number 4 is one of high drama. Assembled by their cabin stewards and directed by the ship's officers, a small group of influential passengers gathered at around 12.30 am on A deck's forward port side, beneath boat 4's davits but behind the glassed-in deck enclosure.

Thayers, Wideners, Ryersons, Astors. . . Husbands, wives and families, some with maids and valets: men and women accustomed to giving orders, not taking them. Now, however, they waited patiently, almost humbly, for the lifeboat to be lowered from the deck above. The lifejackets and light clothing they had hurriedly donned gave scant protection from the chill air. As the minutes passed some of the ladies sent their maids back for warmer clothing: fur coats for the women, warm sweaters or jackets for the men. And still they waited.

After swinging out number 4, Lightoller ordered it lowered to A deck, intending to load passengers through the deck screen's windows. But no-one from the deck crew could be diverted to open them. After about half an hour, shortly after 1 am, second steward George Dodd directed the group to climb the steep stairway forward (its small brass plaque bearing the admonition 'These stairs for use of crew only') to the boat deck.

Since other boats were loaded from the boat deck, the crew might have thought that boat 4 would be hoisted back up and loaded in the same way. Again the passengers waited, now with the sound of the unseen ship's orchestra coming to them across the deckhouse roofs from the starboard side, with the hiss, flare and booming explosions of the distress rockets proclaiming the situation's urgency. Around them they could see people boarding other boats which were then lowered. But still they waited beside the davits whose falls held number 4 captive against the side of A deck, below.

Finding that passengers could be loaded and lowered conveniently from the boat deck, Lightoller finally realised that passengers for boat 4 were still awaiting loading. Once again the Thayers, Wideners, Astors, Ryersons and their entourages were herded back down to A deck. By now the windows had been cranked open, but another problem became evident. *Titanic*'s port list created a gap between the ship's side and the dangling boat. This condition was remedied by pulling the boat inwards with boat-hooks and temporarily securing it with a wire hawser normally used for coaling.

A makeshift step-ladder was rigged up. The women mounted the narrow treads and awkwardly climbed through the windows, from the lighted deck to the outside darkness. Thirteen-year-old Jack Ryerson at first was prevented from accompanying his mother, but his father's appeal overruled the loading officer's objection.

Legend reports that John Jacob Astor, standing nearby, placed a woman's hat on young Ryerson's head, saying, 'There, now you're a girl and you can go'. But the story was not repeated in Mrs Ryerson's later affidavit. (Another legend attributed to Astor tells how, standing at the bar after the collision, he said, 'I asked for ice, but this is ridiculous'. This story is quite unlikely since Astor never was famous for his humour.)

Astor did assist his five-months pregnant wife into the lifeboat, then asked the officer in charge if he might accompany her. After being refused, Astor joined the other gentlemen on deck in assisting ladies into the boat. They assured their wives they would soon follow in other boats, that nearby liners were on the way, that the women were to obey the ship's crewmen and not to worry. Astor stood on deck smiling, waving gently as finally, at 1.55 am, boat 4 was lowered to the sea. Astor's final heroic act was to descend quickly to the dog kennels on F deck, next to the third class galley. (One wonders if he might have heard the roar of the onrushing water as it filled the nearest watertight compartment.) There, he liberated his Airedale dog, Kitty. Madeleine Astor later reported that as she looked back, trying to glimpse her husband, she saw Kitty running about the deck as *Titanic* settled, bow down, lower and lower. . .

Lifeboat number 4 was lowered to the promenade deck just before 1 am. But more than an hour's wait ensued until seamen could be spared to crank open the glass windows allowing access. John Jacob Astor assisted his 19-year-old wife of seven months into the boat, which was two-thirds full. Refusing a seat himself, Astor stepped back, casually lit a cigarette and bravely waved good-bye to Madeleine as the boat was lowered away. A legend was born. (New York American.)

Including hands there were 32 persons aboard boat 4 as it descended. It had taken so long to load that its downward journey was a mere 25 feet rather than the 70 feet it normally would have travelled from A deck. Past the lighted portholes the boat was lowered, past portholes through which water flowed in. On reaching the water only a single seaman had been found aboard (the other crew being storekeepers and firemen); quartermaster Walter Perkis slid down the fall and into the boat where he took charge.

It was now after 2 am. *Titanic*'s bow buried itself deeper with every minute. Boat 4, the last to leave, was just a ship's length away when, following the sinking, it picked up eight crew members from the sea. Two of these later died in the boat. After sighting *Carpathia* about fives miles away, boat 4 reached the rescue ship's side at about 7.30 am.

While lifeboat 4's story unfolded, tales from other boats were no less dramatic. . .

Generally on the port side only women and children were allowed in boats, while on the starboard side men could board if no women were present. Between 12.45 am, when the first boat — starboard number 7 — was lowered, and 2.20 am, when collapsible boats A and B floated off the sinking liner, 698 survivors managed to board boats and safely leave the ship. (Following the sinking fourteen people, mostly crew but including one woman passenger, Rosa Abbott, were pulled from the water; of these, only seven survived.)

Titanic had been planned to accommodate 2,435 passengers and 860 crew, a total of 3,295. On her maiden voyage she carried just 2,228. Yet the antiquated Board of Trade regulations, based on cubic footage, required a lifeboat capacity for only 980 people. *Titanic*'s lifeboat capacity was 1,176. The extra seating for 196 provided by her four collapsible boats was more than ten per cent beyond statutory requirements.

Titanic carried fourteen lifeboats, with a capacity of 65 each, giving 910 seats in total; two emergency cutters, each for 35 persons, or 70 in all; and the four collapsibles, each capable of carrying 49, providing 196 additional seats.

Yet only four *Titanic* boats were lowered carrying anywhere near their full capacities; of the remaining sixteen only three had more than fifty people aboard. Not including collapsibles A and B, which floated off, the average number aboard the remaining eighteen boats was a startling 44. But even loaded to total capacity, with every available seat occupied, 1,052 people would still have lost their lives even under the most ideal circumstances.

As the boats were filled and carefully lowered the great drama ran its inevitable course. The first boats were less than half-filled, their occupants boarding reluctantly, perhaps a bit ashamed of demonstrating so little faith in the liner's safety. But as minutes passed the danger began to dawn upon passengers and crew alike. More and more people crowded to the edge of the boat deck, the pushing becoming stronger until near-panic ensued.

Under Captain Smith's orders, fourth officer Boxhall fired the first distress rocket at about 12.45 am as the first lifeboat (number 7) was lowered. Far aft, walking his lonely watch at the stern, quartermaster George Rowe saw the boat slip past. Unaware of the evacuation, Rowe rang the bridge. He was ordered to gather additional percussive rockets and report immediately to the navigating bridge. Once there, he assisted Boxhall in firing rockets until 1.25 (Rowe may have been a bit off in his reckoning: Boxhall later stated that he kept 'sending the rockets up right to the very last minute I was sent away in the boat', number 2, which left at 1.45 am.)

Shortly before 1 am Bruce Ismay tried to assist fifth officer Lowe in putting boat 5 into the water. 'Lower away, lower away!' he called as he waved his arm in circles. Lowe could not stand the interference. 'Get the hell out of the way,' he shouted, 'and I'll lower away. Do you want me to drown the lot of them?' Abashed, Ismay turned and without a word quickly walked forward to boat 3.

Port boat 6 was also being lowered at about this time. Mrs James Joseph Brown (better known as 'Molly') was walking away from it to see what was being done elsewhere, having persuaded several of her more timid friends to board. Suddenly she was roughly seized by two acquaintances, Edward Calderhead and James McGough, and dumped over the side, falling four feet into the already-descending boat. There were just two seamen, Fleet and Hichens, in the boat and as they reached the water Molly made good use of her loud voice to demand another sailor. Major Arthur Godfrey Peuchen, a yachtsman, volunteered and was permitted by second officer Lightoller to join the boat. Swinging more than six feet out to the falls and then rapidly descending hand-over-hand more than 60 feet, Peuchen was soon aboard.

The boat now in the water, Hichens refused to row. Peuchen and Fleet were not strong enough together to row the heavily loaded boat. Doffing her lifejacket, Molly Brown seized an oar and, through her example, soon had some of the 24 other women 'manning' the boat. Later, when they were able to take another man aboard — a stoker from boat 16 — Mrs Brown wrapped the thinly clad man in her own fur coat and very likely saved his life. Throughout the ordeal her cheerfulness and strength of character did much to prevent panic.

Even though first officer Murdoch permitted men to enter starboard boat number 3,

During the lowering of the lifeboats, Ida Straus, wife of New York millionaire Isidor Straus, was urged to enter the boat. But she refused to do so without her husband who, in turn, would not board until all women had been embarked. The two were last seen as they left the deck to meet their fate together. (Authors' collection.)

there were several gentlemen who, after assisting ladies into the boat, stood away and went elsewhere, to be lost: Messrs Case, Hays, Davidson and Roebling were men who had much to live for, men who saw their duty and did it unselfishly and superbly.

As portside boat 8 was loading, Isidor and Ida Straus, together with Mrs Straus's maid Ellen Bird, approached the boat. Miss Bird got in, but Mr Straus refused to board until all women and children were safe. Mrs Straus would not leave without her husband. When last seen the two elderly people were re-entering the ship, perhaps to go below to meet their fate together.

At about the same time that the Strauses were, so unselfishly, leaving space in their boat for others, starboard boat number 1, one of the two emergency cutters, was readying for launch. First officer Murdoch ordered several firemen to enter the boat.

First class passengers Sir Cosmo and Lady Lucile Duff-Gordon, with the latter's secretary Miss Laura Francatelli, appeared and asked if they might enter the boat. Seeing no others — men or women — around, Murdoch helped the group into the boat, along with two American gentlemen who had just arrived. There were still no others — men, women or crew — in sight as Murdoch gave the order to lower away. And boat 1, capacity 35, reached the water with five passengers and seven crew aboard.

Later, following the sinking, while the cries of the freezing and the drowning rang in their ears, the boat's occupants refused to return to the disaster site for fear they would be swamped. Look-out George Symons, nominally in charge, kept his mouth shut. And no-one objected when Lady Duff-Gordon suggested they should not return. The boat reached *Carpathia* with its twelve-member party comfortably intact. Subsequently, Sir Cosmo provided each crew member with a five pound cheque, ostensibly to replace their lost kits. . .

Now as the situation's urgency became apparent, port boat 10 left with 55 aboard. There were 56 aboard starboard boat 9 as it, too, left at 1.20 am. As port boat 12 was lowered away, famed novelist and mystery writer Jacques Futrelle stood back and waved good-bye to his wife. Less than six days earlier, on the evening of 9 April, the two had celebrated Jacques' 37th birthday at a fashionable London restaurant. . .

Boats 11 and 13 were lowered to A deck and loaded at almost the same time. Stewards formed a human chain and hurriedly passed women and children across the deck and into the boats. For one woman, an ordeal began that ultimately would be resolved by *Carpathia*'s Captain Arthur Rostron. As she awaited her turn to board, third class passenger Mrs Leah Aks was astonished to have her ten-month-old son Frank torn from her protective grasp. Struggling to regain hold of her baby, Mrs Aks was pushed aside by the stewards, who believed she was 'rushing the boat'.

Frank Phillip Aks, or as he was nicknamed, Filly, was tossed roughly into the nearly-loaded boat. He was caught — much like a football — by Elizabeth Nye, who clutched the wailing baby in her lap, later wrapping him in a brown plaid steamer blanket to protect him from the cold.

In Frank Aks' own words, 'My mother was in a state of shock, having lost her baby. She was pushed into lifeboat number 13 next to Mrs Selena Rogers Cook. She was a warm, compassionate woman, comforting and watching over my mother throughout the night and during the transfer to and aboard the *Carpathia*.

'My mother and Mrs Rogers were sitting on the *Carpathia*'s deck when a woman passed by with a baby in her arms; that baby was me! When I saw my mother I immediately stretched out my arms toward her. [But] Elizabeth Nye claimed me as her own. Mrs Rogers went to Captain Rostron of the *Carpathia* with my mother and told him the story.

'He took the two ladies and me to his quarters. Proof of identification was made through a strawberry birthmark under my left breast. I was returned to my mother'.

At 1.25 am starboard boats 11 and 13 were lowered almost simultaneously — 11 with 70 aboard, 13 with 64. Also among those in boat 11 were eight-year-old Marshall Drew and his Aunt Lulu. He vividly recalled the evacuation not long before his passing in 1986:

> 'At 11.40 pm April 14th when the *Titanic* struck the iceberg, I was in bed. However, for whatever reason I was awake and remember the jolt and cessation of motion.
>
> 'A steward knocked on the stateroom door and directed us to get dressed, put on life preservers and go to the boat deck, which we did.
>
> 'There was a watertight compartment door next to our stateroom. As we left it was closed.
>
> 'I remember the steward as we passed was trying to arouse passengers who had locked themselves in for the night.
>
> 'Elevators were not running. We walked up to the boat deck. All was calm and orderly. An officer was in charge. "Women and children first," [he said] as he directed lifeboat number 11 to be filled. There were many tearful farewells. We and Uncle Jim said "Good bye".
>
> 'Waiting on deck before this I could hear the ship's orchestra playing somewhere off toward first class.

'Lifeboat number 11 was near the stern. I will never forget that as I looked over my right shoulder, [the] steerage [promenade area] was blacked out. It made an impression I never forgot.

'Now I know from reading that lifeboat number 11 was the only lifeboat filled to capacity. The lowering of the lifeboat seventy feet to the sea was perilous. Davits, ropes, nothing worked properly so that first one end of the lifeboat was tilted up and then far down. I think it was the only time I was scared.

'Lifeboats pulled some distance away from the sinking *Titanic*, afraid of what suction might do. I am always annoyed at artists' depictions of the sinking *Titanic*. I've never seen one that came anywhere near the truth. There might have been the slightest ocean swell but it was dead calm. Stars there may have been, but the blackness of the night was so intense one could not see anything like a horizon. . .'

As it neared the water, boat 13 was almost swamped by a large stream of water being discharged from *Titanic*'s side by the labouring pumps deep within the hull.

Below left *Lifeboat 13, with 54 of her 64 occupants women, was lowered at 1.25 am. Less than a minute later, the adjacent boat 15 was lowered. Boat 13 reached the water, but before her falls could be severed, she was washed beneath the descending boat 15. Disaster seemed imminent, but the falls were cut and boat 13 drifted clear just in time. (*Daily Graphic.*)*

Below right *Around 1.30 am when the ship's foundering seemed inevitable, Benjamin Guggenheim and his valet Victor Giglio appeared on deck in full evening dress. They had shed the heavy sweaters and lifejackets worn earlier. In Mr Guggenheim's words, 'We've dressed in our best and are prepared to go down like gentlemen'. Another legend was generated. (*New York Times.*)*

Boat 13's safety was threatened further when it reached the water. It drifted astern before its falls could be cut and was nearly crushed under boat 15, lowered moments after 13 with seventy aboard (almost all third class women and children). Boat 13's falls were cut barely in time to prevent a vertical collision.

Port boat 14 with sixty aboard was lowered at 1.30. As fifth officer Lowe assisted the more than fifty women aboard he flourished his gun to keep back the surrounding men who threatened to rush the boat. Lowe himself got in as the boat was lowered, not so much to take command as to keep an eye out for it as well as boats 12 and 14 which were lowered almost simultaneously. Once afloat, Lowe mustered boats 10, 12, collapsible D and 4 near his own number 14. Tying them together, Lowe oversaw transfer of crew and passengers between boats to balance their loads. He later rigged a mast and sail aboard number 14, to propel the flotilla towards the approaching *Carpathia*.

In the forward davits used to launch boat 1 now hung collapsible C, loading under first officer Murdoch's direction. The boat was already almost two-thirds full when a large group of men appeared ready to rush the boat. Chief purser Herbert McElroy, assisting Murdoch, fired his pistol twice and the sound so startled the incipient mob that the men fell back, leaving a wide space around the boat.

Seeing no women nearby, Wilde ordered the boat to be lowered. It began to move below deck level, and seeing no-one else in its vicinity, J. Bruce Ismay stepped quietly and quickly forward, boarding the boat as it descended. This act, while scarcely a cowardly one under the immediate circumstances, was later to cause him many agonized hours of intense regret.

As the bow dipped ever lower in the icy Atlantic water, there were those who stood fast and performed their duty as they saw it, those whose courage and bravery shine as bright stars against disaster's dark fabric. . .

Among them were the men who helped to load women and children into the lifeboats,

Travelling with his two sons, second class passenger 'Mr Hoffman' was actually Michel Navratil, who kidnapped the children in an effort to rescue a failing marriage. Shortly before 2 am he handed his two sons to second officer Lightoller through the ring of crewmen formed to protect the last boat, Collapsible D, from being swamped by the more than 1,500 still aboard. (Harper's.)

and who then stood away as the boats were lowered, even though there were empty seats. . .

The 34 engineering officers — engineers, electricians, plumbers, boiler room personnel — who maintained electricity and lighting until almost the final moment. Of these brave men who laboured amid heat, sound, hot metal and shifting coal not one deserted his post, not one was saved.

In his fitting tribute to these courageous men. Lord Beresford wrote, 'Had it not been for their steadfast dedication to duty, many more lives would have been lost'. His Majesty King George V agreed, decreeing that henceforth British marine engineers would wear their rank insignia against a royal purple background, as a remembrance of their brave *Titanic* colleagues. . .

One must not forget the gallant postal clerks, five men, neither White Star employees nor *Titanic* crew members, men entrusted by their governments with the safety of the mails. Two British, three American citizens whose department forward on G deck's starboard side was among the first areas to be flooded. Within five minutes the water had sloshed around their knees as they dragged 200 sacks of registered mail from the storage room on the orlop deck to the dryer G deck sorting room. Their efforts were in vain. Even before the last sack arrived, water had already risen to that level. Continuing to struggle with the heavy sacks, sometimes enlisting help from several available stewards, the clerks then pulled their precious bags of registered mail up the steep inside stairways to the starboard side corridor of D deck's forward cabins. They hoped to off-load the mail through the first class entrance, just aft of that area. It was a forlorn hope.

In the words of the Brooklyn (New York) *Daily Eagle*,

> 'The Brooklyn mail clerk [William Logan Gwinn] was then with the other four clerks, Oscar S. Woody of Washington, DC, John Starr March of Newark, NJ, John Richard Jago Smith and James Bertram Williamson of England. They were still working over their mail bags, cool and self-contained, until the explosion came and the darkness and the ocean swallowed them up. Not once did they waver or blanch from their duty. Not one can say that they attempted to get into the lifeboats or thought of themselves for a single instant. They stuck to that which their governments had entrusted to their care, and with it they died.'

It is estimated that 3,364 bags of mail and between 700 and 800 parcels were lost in *Titanic*'s sinking. But the tradition of trust and responsibility for the safety of the mails never saw a prouder hour.

The bandsmen. . . Much has been spoken and written concerning these valiant men's actions and behaviour. To recount in detail their last night almost would be superfluous. Memorials (more than for any other segment of the ship's company) have sustained the gallant eight's memory through the years. As long as music is performed, as long as hymns are sung, their heroism will endure: Brailey, Bricoux, Clarke, Hume, Krins, Taylor,

Woodward — and their leader, Wallace Hartley.

Shortly after midnight the orchestra (tradition would have the group called a 'band') assembled in the forward first class entrance, where passengers began gathering before going to the boats. The band's music established a quick bright tempo which kept the passengers' feet moving to its beat. Suspicion, even panic, was quickly averted by the musicians' presence. ('Why, if they're playing here, things can't be *that* bad.')

Later, when passengers had stepped out on to the promenade and boat decks, the band reassembled outside the gymnasium near the first class entrance's starboard side. Around 12.45 am, as the first lifeboat, number 7, was lowered, they began playing a brave counterpoint to the sound of shuffling feet and the increasing murmur of confused passengers. The music helped bring order to the proceedings.

Their repertoire of marches, quicksteps and occasional waltz tunes was performed with cold-stiffened fingers through the next hour and twenty minutes. As the decks' pitch grew steeper there was no effort to leave. Even those without instruments, pianists Taylor and Brailey, remained with their comrades.

When, at around 2.10 am, the end was very near, bandmaster Hartley advised his men that they had done their duty and could save themselves if they wished. Not one man moved. They stood together on the slanting deck and, struggling to maintain footing, played a hymn, a solemn, soaring requiem to a great ship and its doomed people. . .

Through the years there has been considerable speculation regarding the last music *Titanic*'s bandsmen played. Recollections have ranged from 'Londonderry Air' through the two tunes for the hymn, 'Nearer, My God, to Thee', a sentimental waltz 'Songe d'Automne', and yet another hymn (with its roots in a 1551 setting for a Psalm), 'Autumn'.

Some iconoclasts bravely suggest that *no* music was played or sung as the ship sank. They may be correct: the decks' steep incline at this point would preclude sure footing. And the sound of their music, if indeed they could have played, would have been drowned out by the roar of equipment and furnishings plunging towards the bow. Most references are made to music played immediately before the ship stood on end, broke in two and sank.

For many years there have been strong supporters of the hymn 'Autumn', which surviving telegraphist Harold Bride reported hearing while he struggled in the ocean to save himself, indeed while trapped for some time beneath overturned collapsible B, his ears filled with water. Bride's supporters claim he was a trained technician, alert to his environment, better able than most to observe and remember. His story, related to a New York reporter, received wide coverage. In the emotions generated by the momentous event, the music *could* be accepted as representing the occasion's nobility and dignity.

Some doubt can be cast when one vainly searches for any other person — passenger or crew — who recalls 'Autumn' as the final music. Credibility is strained further when one examines the hymn's tune. Its progressions and intervals do not lend themselves to *ad libitum* performance. ('Autumn' is not listed in the White Star Line's musicians' songbook for 1912.)

The sentiments expressed in the verses are noble ones: 'God of mercy and compassion, look with pity on my pain. . .' and 'Hold me up in mighty waters, keep mine eyes on things above. . .' But there is good cause to doubt the tradition. The words do fulfil requirements of Victorian/Edwardian sentiment and resigned acceptance of calamity. Yet neither the hymn's tune nor its full lyrics lend themselves to singing, playing or recitation during stressful moments save, perhaps, by professional choirmasters. If there were just a single additional witness to Harold Bride's recollection there might be grounds for reconsideration. But there is none. . .

A far better candidate for the 'last music' is the hymn, 'Nearer, My God, to Thee', although some doubt exists as to which *tune* was played. Was it 'Bethany' or 'Horbury'? (For those who have seen both major *Titanic* films, 'Bethany' is used in the 1953 American film *Titanic*, while 'Horbury' was sung in the 1958 British film *A Night to Remember*.)

A British ensemble performing aboard a British ship would have played 'Horbury'. Yet, Americans survivors described the hymn which *they* knew as 'Nearer, My God, to Thee'. And 'Bethany' was the tune familiar to them. Further, there was widespread acceptance and use of 'Bethany' during the many post-disaster memorial concerts.

Might it be possible that bandmaster Hartley, aware of the many Americans aboard *Titanic*, and as a professional familiar with both tunes, selected 'Bethany' as a courtesy to the Americans' sensitivities?

Regardless of the tune, the hymn itself was more than likely the 'last music'. It was known to have been Hartley's favourite hymn. Indeed, when queried by one of his colleagues earlier, while both were playing in *Mauretania*'s band, Hartley stated that if he were aboard a sinking ship he would assemble his men and play either 'O God Our Help in Ages Past' or 'Nearer, My God, to Thee', as both were his favourites. The hymn had also been a great favourite of the late King Edward VII. And it was the hymn played at the graveside of all departed brothers of the Musicians' Union.

Perhaps the most telling quality is its ease of performance and harmonising in an *ad lib* playing of the simple, almost chorale-like melody, a style for which the intricacies of 'Autumn' emphatically were not suited.

It was the American survivors who recalled the hymn and its tune. Their cumulative recollections remained unchallenged at the time by the press on both sides of the Atlantic, but for Bride's lone exception.

In the absence of proven fact (in this case, direct testimony by an orchestra member), and in view of the many conflicting statements, one cannot state with certainty the tune, or even the title, of the last music. The speculation itself represents one of *Titanic*'s many fascinating unproven and unprovable facts.

One irrefutable fact, however, remains: the musicians stayed until all hope of rescue was gone. Who can say how many lives their efforts saved? The final moments of how many were cheered or ennobled by their music? 'Songe d'Automne' or 'Autumn'. 'Horbury' or 'Bethany'. What difference? The memory of the bandsmen and their courageous music will never die.

2.10 am — The water had done its work. Flowing over the watertight bulkheads, filling

Senior wireless operator John G. Phillips (left) and junior operator Harold S. Bride (right) heroically stood at their post until moments before Titanic *finally sank, bravely transmitting signals. (Marconi Marine.)*

one compartment after another, the water's weight had pulled *Titanic*'s bow completely under. As the seconds passed the huge liner's immense bulk started a catastrophic arc into the black diamond-point sky.

As energy from the dynamos faltered, the last wireless signal spluttered to a halt: ' - - - - - - - - - ' and then no more.

Marshall Drew recalled *Titanic*'s end:

'As row by row of the porthole lights of the *Titanic* sank into the sea this was about all one could see. When the *Titanic* upended to sink, all was blacked out until the tons of machinery crashed to the bow. This sounded like an explosion, which of course it was not.

'As this happened the hundreds and hundreds of people were thrown into the sea. It isn't likely I shall ever forget the screams of these people as they perished in water said to be 28 degrees.'

2.15 am — *Titanic*'s stern rose higher and higher. Inside the ship all furnishings and fittings, tableware, glasses, dishes, everything movable began to slide towards the bow. In a cacophonous blur of thunder every unattached chair, bed, lamp, every table and sofa followed.

By 2.18 the lights assured by the engineers' brave sacrifice finally glowed red, flickered once, twice, then went out, leaving *Titanic*'s curved hull blacker against the night's blackness, her three great propellers dripping streams of water once clear of their accustomed element.

The arc reached its full extent; *Titanic* stood almost vertically for ten. . . twenty. . . thirty seconds.

2.20 am — With the bow well under water, the remaining hull slipped downwards with a heavy gurgling sound. As they reached the water the funnels broke off one by one, sending clouds of soot and steam gushing into the air. The four funnels themselves, crushed and broken, planed off in as many directions.

Not yet fully under the surface, the tortured hull broke with a mighty roar near the after expansion joint and an engine room airshaft. The forward section, three-fifths of the ship, planed away toward the ocean floor. The stern section, containing the immense triple-expansion engines and the heavy turbine, together weighing more than 1,000 tons, remained afloat a few seconds more, then lost its buoyancy and plummeted straight to the bottom. A burst of compressed air rose explosively to the surface in a single bubble, so close to the sinking site as to appear part of it.

The stern followed the direction taken by the bow, pirouetting slowly as it sank further. . .

On the surface the black water was marbled with white-bubbled spume rising from the broken hulk. Debris torn from the hull's fractures bobbed to the surface. Soon there was a trail of it marking the sinking liner's direction.

Twenty boats, one overturned, another awash, floated in the glass-like sea. A mile or more away floated a great iceberg which resembled the Rock of Gibraltar, a smear of red and black paint running along its base. . .

Over the sea's surface the cries for help sounded loudly at first, then more faintly, until there was nothing. . .nothing but 'twenty boats and a quiet sea', and silence.

As the sounds ebbed, childhood fascination with what was occurring around him gave way to ennui. Marshall Drew recalled:

> 'The reader will have to understand that at this point in my life I was being brought up as a typical British kid. You were not allowed to cry. You were a "little man". So! As a cool kid I lay down in the bottom of the lifeboat and went to sleep.
>
> 'When I awoke it was broad daylight as we approached the *Carpathia*. Looking around over the gunwale it seemed to me like the Arctic. Icebergs of huge size ringed the horizon for 360 degrees.'

Nowhere is *Titanic*'s sinking so vividly described as by those who experienced the frightful disaster. And nowhere is the picture so graphically represented as when seen through a child's eyes.

Another youngster on board was twelve-year-old Ruth Becker. Written in her mature years (now as Mrs Ruth Blanchard), this account recalls the hours of cold and uncertainty spent in *Titanic*'s boats. It is published here by Mrs Blanchard's kind permission:

'As our lifeboat number 13 pulled out from the side of the *Titanic* we could see the water rushing into the ship. Rowing away, looking at the *Titanic*, it was a beautiful sight outlined against the starry sky, every port hole and saloon blazing with light. It was impossible to think anything could be wrong with such an enormous ship, were it not for the tilt downward towards the bow. . . Finally as the *Titanic* sank faster, the lights in the cabins and saloons died out. At the same time the machinery roared down through the vessel with a rattle and a groaning that could be heard for miles — the weirdest sound, surely, that could be heard in the middle of the ocean, a thousand miles from land.

'To our amazement the *Titanic* seemed to break in half, the prow slipping down quietly under the waters, and the stern remaining in an upright position for a couple of minutes, seeming to say, "Good bye — so sorry!"

'Then with a quiet slanting dive it disappeared beneath the waters, and our eyes looked for the last time on the gigantic vessel we had set out on from Southampton last Wednesday.

'Such a tragedy! Over 2,000 people on board, plenty of time to get off, but 1,500 persons went down with the ship because there were only 20 lifeboats available, definitely not enough to accommodate every man, woman and child.

'Lifeboat number 13 that I was in had about 65 people in it so it was filled to standing room with men and women in every conceivable condition of dress and undress. It was bitter cold — a curious, deadening, bitter cold. And then with all of this, there fell on the ear the most terrible noises that human beings ever listened to — the cries of hundreds of people struggling in the icy cold water, crying for help with a cry that we knew could not be answered. We wanted to pick up some of those swimming, but this would have meant swamping our boat and further loss of the lives of all of us.

'It was not until then that I realized that I was still holding on to the blankets I had brought up from our cabin. In the rush I had forgotten to give them to my mother to wrap around my brother, two years old, and sister, four years old. [They had left *Titanic* in another lifeboat.] The men who were rowing our boat were stokers. They had been working near the bottom of the ship near the boilers when the *Titanic* struck. Therefore, when the ship was ripped open, the water rushed in and soaked all of them. They escaped with nothing on except sleeveless shirts and shorts. So you can imagine how cold they were out in that freezing weather. The officer in charge asked me to give up my blankets to wrap around these men, which I gladly did. Also, the finger on one of the men was almost cut off. I happened to find a large handkerchief — my father's — in my coat pocket. So we tore that in strips and wrapped them around his finger.

'Standing on one side of me was a little German lady. She was crying [and] I asked her why. She told me — through an interpreter standing near — that her little six-weeks-old baby had been taken away from her on the *Titanic* and put into another boat. The baby was wrapped so heavily in blankets that she was afraid it would be taken for baggage and thrown in the ocean. All excess baggage was thrown overboard.

'All lifeboats were supposed to be equipped with oars, a compass, a light, and food (crackers). Our lifeboat had only oars. The other boats seemed to be in the same predicament because we were all scattered. But we were very lucky. The captain of the boat said he had been at sea for 26 years and had never yet seen such a calm night on the Atlantic.

'We all, of course, were watching for the light of a rescue ship. Finally about 4 o'clock in the morning we did see a light which came closer and closer. Rockets were being sent up and the foghorn kept blowing and blowing.

'You can imagine our joy because we knew it must be a rescue ship. All of us shouted and yelled. We were really happy because the sea was getting choppy and that was the first time I was a little concerned. Our tiny boat bounced around like a cork. The *Carpathia*, our rescue ship, stopped. We rowed to it, and our boat load was rescued.'

TWO
Lights that Pass in the Night

After checking on the damage forward, *Titanic*'s fourth officer Boxhall had reported his findings to Captain Smith on the bridge. Then, at about midnight, he roused officers Lightoller and Pitman, still in their respective cabins awaiting orders.

Boxhall next went along the port side seeing to the unlacing of boat covers. As he reached the bridge again he was intercepted by the captain and ordered to work out *Titanic*'s position. Entering the chart room he quickly established a position and took his conclusions to Captain Smith, who, he later said, told him to take the position to the Marconi room. (In his American inquiry testimony, telegraphist Harold Bride stated specifically that Captain Smith had brought in the position report.)

It was as he returned to the bridge from the Marconi room, Boxhall told the Board of Trade inquiry, that he first saw the light of a ship near *Titanic*. He stated that with binoculars he distinctly could make out the ship's two masthead lights.

At about 12.45 am Boxhall fired off the first distress rocket. As he continued to do so at about five-minute intervals with quartermaster George Rowe's assistance, he observed the ship approaching. Soon he was able to discern her red port sidelight and her green starboard lamp without binoculars.

The lights were observed by others on the bridge, including the captain. They first appeared about half a point on *Titanic*'s port bow. Presently the approaching vessel's red port light, alone, could be seen. Captain Smith ordered Boxhall and Rowe to try contacting the vessel with the morse lamp, and they did so in between firing rockets. Rowe later judged that the ship was four or five miles away, while Boxhall thought the distance five or six miles. There was no response from the other vessel to either the overwhelming din of the distress rockets or to the powerful morse signal lamp. She seemed to be turning slowly; just before Boxhall departed from *Titanic*'s bridge at about 1.40 am (to join number 2 boat, lowered at 1.45 am), he observed only the vessel's stern light, now two points off *Titanic*'s bow. It seemed to Boxhall that, in spite of frantic morse lamp and rocket signals, the other vessel was sailing off.

(It should be noted that *Titanic* was stationary in the water. She was drifting with the southerly current, but not turning. What Boxhall emphatically and realistically describes, augmented by quartermaster Rowe's observations, is a vessel that approached, passed about two points off *Titanic*'s bow at a distance of five miles, then turned and sailed away — *a moving ship*.)

(1)   (2)

More than 19 miles from the sinking Titanic *the Leyland freighter had been stopped by ice since 7.30 pm. Hours later, her crew saw the lights of a vessel less than eight miles distant. While* Californian's *Captain Stanley Lord (1) dozed in the chart room and her radio operator Cyril Evans (2) was off duty, donkeyman Ernest Gill (3) thought he saw the nearby vessel throwing rockets. Third officer Charles V. Groves (4) tried unsuccessfully to signal the ship which he later described as a small tramp steamer five to eight miles away. (*Washington Evening Star; New York American; Boston Journal; Daily Sketch.)

(3)   (4)

At about 12.45, while loading boat number 6 which left at 12.55, second officer Lightoller also had observed a light about two points off *Titanic*'s port bow. The light did not move. Indeed, Lightoller recalled encouraging the frightened passengers by telling them he thought the light was a sailing vessel, and that later in the morning when the wind came up, the vessel would come and pick up the people in the boats. While Lightoller continued observing the vessel's light between his many duties, it did not appear to move.

The Leyland Line's cargo vessel *Californian* departed from Liverpool on 5 April for Boston, Massachusetts with a general cargo aboard. By 14 April her noon position, by observation, was 42°05′ N, 47°25′ W. During the afternoon her course was altered after ice reports were received on 9 and 13 April. At 6.30 pm three large bergs were sighted and *Californian*'s captain, Stanley Lord, ordered wireless operator Cyril Evans to advise the Leyland freighter *Antillian*, then in communications range, of the ice.

At 7.30 pm *Californian*'s chief officer George F. Stewart took an observation on the Pole Star and reported to Captain Lord a latitude of 42°5½′ N. Because of his vessel's proximity to ice, Lord doubled his look-outs at 8 pm and later took charge of the bridge himself, third officer Charles Groves also being on duty. At 10.15 there was a brightening on the western horizon and Lord concluded that this 'glow' was caused by ice. At 10.21 he ordered the ship to be stopped and the helm put hard a-port. *Californian* swung around to the east-north-east by compass (north-east true) and came to a halt.

Stopped in loose ice about half a mile from the edge of a low ice-field, Lord calculated the vessel's position and entered it in the log: 42°05′ N, 50°07′ W.

When he left the bridge at 10.30 to go below Captain Lord pointed out to the third officer a light to the eastward. Lord thought it was an approaching vessel. Groves thought it was a star. As he returned to the bridge around 10.55 Lord encountered the wireless operator and asked him if he knew of any other vessels in the vicinity. 'Only *Titanic*,' responded Evans.

'That's not *Titanic*. She's closer to us in size,' replied Lord, indicating the slowly approaching ship. 'You'd better contact *Titanic* anyway and let her know we're stopped in ice.' Wireless operator Evans went immediately to send the message.

By 11.30 pm the other ship's green starboard light could be seen. Lord, still on the bridge, estimated her distance at about five miles and asked that she be contacted by morse lamp. There was no response from the other vessel, however.

At the midnight watch change Captain Lord asked the relieving watch officer, second officer Herbert Stone, to advise him if the nearby vessel came any closer. He told Stone that he would be resting on the chart room's settee and left the bridge.

To Stone the vessel appeared to be to the south-south-east and dead abeam, starboard of *Californian*. He observed one masthead light and a red sidelight, as well as one or two indistinct lights resembling open doors or portholes. He judged her to be a small tramp steamer about five miles off.

Like Groves earlier, Stone repeatedly tried morsing the ship, beginning at about 12.10, but also without success.

Around midnight fireman Ernest Gill came on deck after completing his 8-to-12 watch. Having just come from the lighted engine room, Gill blinked his eyes against the night's darkness as he leaned over the starboard rail of *Californian*'s upper deck. Peering into the night Gill saw '. . . a very large steamer, about ten miles away. I watched her for a full minute. . . She was going at full speed'. Gill went below but was unable to sleep. He left his bunk and went up on deck again about 12.30 am. He had been there for about ten minutes when he saw a white rocket, '. . .about ten miles away on the starboard side. I thought it must be a shooting star. In seven or eight minutes I saw distinctly a second rocket in the same place. . . It was not my business to notify the bridge or the look-outs. . . I turned in immediately after'.

At the subsequent American inquiry Gill reported that while he could see stars spangling out from the rockets, he observed no morse signalling from the vessel, nor could he hear any noise such as escaping steam, concussions from exploding distress rockets, or anything of the sort, though conditions that night were ideal for doing so, especially from the ten-mile distance about which he was so positive.

On the bridge second officer Stone also had observed a flash of light in the sky at about 12.45 am, *Californian*'s time. He then thought nothing of it for several shooting stars had already been plainly sighted. But a short time later he viewed another light, directly over the nearby steamer, appearing to come from a good distance beyond her. Between that time and about 1.15 am he observed three more lights, the same as before and all white in colour.

At 1.15 Stone whistled down the speaking tube to advise Captain Lord of the rockets. Answering from his own cabin, Lord inquired if the rockets were company signals. Stone replied, 'I don't know, but they're all white'. Lord ordered Stone to continue signalling the nearby vessel via morse lamp, and '. . .when you do [get an answer], let me know by Gibson'. Again Stone signalled the ship, again without response. The captain returned to the chart room settee.

Californian continued to swing through south and by 1.50 am was heading west-south-west. The other ship had a bearing of south-west-by-west and around 2 am had begun steaming away, bearing SW ½ W. Her red portside light became invisible, and only her stern light could be seen.

As ordered, Stone sent apprentice Gibson to report to the captain. Gibson returned saying he had told the captain not only of the ship's departure but also of the sighting of eight distant rockets. According to Gibson the captain acknowledged his report and then inquired about the rockets: 'Are you sure there were no colours in them?' He then asked Gibson the time and, after telling him, Gibson returned to the bridge to report to Stone. But Lord was unaware of Gibson's visit. In a sworn affidavit he stated, 'I have recollection between 1.30 and 4.30 of Gibson opening the chart room door and closing it immediately. I said "What is it?" but he did not reply'.

Captain Lord was not the only drowsy member of *Californian*'s crew. Telegraphist Cyril Evans, rebuffed by *Titanic*'s operator Jack Phillips during his attempt to contact the liner, had taken off his headphones, shut down his apparatus and gone to bed. His station's mechanically operated detector was unwound, and therefore unresponsive to the distress calls which so soon afterwards began crackling through the night. . .

At first *Carpathia* sped through a smooth sea on her course of North 52 West. By 2.30 am preparations to receive survivors were completed.

A full head of steam from seven boilers drove her two quadruple expansion engines ever faster. *Carpathia*'s normal top speed was 14½ knots. Never again did the ship attain the 17½ knot speed reached during her dash to *Titanic*. Her frame shuddered, her bedplates vibrated as the engines strained to meet the demand of speed, more speed. . .

As *Carpathia* approached *Titanic*'s last radioed position (heard more than a full, ominous hour ago, now), there were icebergs to dodge. But by masterful navigation, Rostron guided his 540 foot liner through the ice while never slackening speed. At 3 am, he ordered rockets to be fired at 15-minute intervals to let survivors know help was approaching. By 3.35 am *Carpathia* had reached almost the exact position where *Titanic*, if afloat, would have been visible. But there was only an empty sea punctuated by bobbing ice.

At 4 o'clock the engines were stopped. About 300 yards ahead a green light shone low in the water. *Carpathia* drifted closer. The lifeboat was alongside. Lines were thrown and made fast. At 4.10 am the women from *Titanic*'s lifeboat 2 began to climb through the shelter deck's open gangway. There were only 25 in a boat designed for 40. Fourth officer Boxhall, ordered to look after the boat's all-female complement, climbed wearily on to *Carpathia*'s deck. Captain Rostron sent word asking him to report to the bridge. Still wet and shivering uncontrollably as much from emotion as cold, Boxhall told Rostron that *Titanic* had sunk at 2.20 am.

One by one the lifeboats drew close to *Carpathia*'s towering sides. Many women were hauled up in slings and bosun's chairs, children in canvas ash bags. The men, crew and passengers alike, climbed slowly up the ladders and nets slung over the side. As they reached deck they were taken below where warmth and nourishment awaited them.

Ruth Becker Blanchard remembered the moment of rescue:

'From the time we knew the *Titanic* had struck the iceberg until the *Carpathia* came to rescue us, I was not afraid. Every minute was exciting to me. I didn't think for a moment that we wouldn't be saved. It was not until the *Titanic* went down with all those people on the decks — screaming and jumping into the water — that I realized the seriousness of it. My mother, brother and sister had been put into a lifeboat before I was, so I knew they had gotten off the ship.

'When we rowed up alongside the *Carpathia*, we discovered that we were so cold we could hardly move. Swings were lowered to take us up. I was the first one to be put in the swing and tied in because I was so numb I couldn't hold on. I was pulled up to the top and taken into the waiting room where the survivors were given brandy and hot coffee. Blankets were piled to the ceiling. I thawed out immediately without the brandy and coffee.

'I had promised the little German lady that I would help her find her baby. I wanted to find my mother, too. Moving around the ship from first to second class, to be sure we didn't miss any of the passengers as they came in, and looking over the deck railing, it seemed like hours had gone by while we watched the lifeboats come in.

'Around 10 o'clock I found my mother. A passenger came up to me and said, "Are you Ruth Becker?" I said, "Yes". She said, "Your mother has been looking all over for you". So she took me to Mother and our family was reunited. The little German lady found her baby, too. I never saw anybody so happy in my life!

'The baby happened to be in my mother's boat. Mother said, "It was lucky the child wasn't thrown overboard because it looked like a bundle of clothes — but just in time it started to cry. When they found that the 'bundle' was a baby, everybody wanted to take care of it". The mother and her baby were meeting her husband in New York City.

'Of course, Mother and I were delighted to see each other. She was a nervous wreck, crying when anybody asked her about her experience. And no wonder! Having the responsibility of taking care of the two little children, and not being sure that I had gotten off the *Titanic*. The experience hadn't affected me emotionally at all, so I answered all questions.'

Carpathia's own passengers lined the decks; stewards had been unable to keep them inside. In the half light of the approaching dawn, they stood mute and uninterfering as *Titanic*'s survivors clambered aboard. There was no sound except the shuffling of feet, an occasional muted sob, a soft word of guidance or support, the squeal of block and tackle as another chair or ash bag was hauled up.

Collapsible C was picked up at 6.15 am. At 7 am boat 14 with fifth officer Lowe in firm command and towing collapsible D was alongside. During the night he had transferred twelve men and one women (Rosa Abbott) from half-swamped collapsible A to collapsible D. Leaving three bodies aboard, Lowe opened boat A's seacocks before setting it adrift.

The breeze Ruth Becker had noticed caused Lightoller difficulty in keeping his overturned boat, collapsible B, afloat and on an even keel. Moving at his command, the two dozen aboard leaned together, first right then left, to keep the balance. The boat was sinking low in the water and Lightoller was afraid that they would not be seen. He repeatedly blew his seaman's whistle to attract attention. Finally *Carpathia* turned towards them, moving slowly now that the wind had begun to influence her own motion. By 8.30 the small boat was alongside and all were taken aboard quickly, including the body of one who had died during the night. Lightoller himself was the last up the ladder, the final *Titanic* survivor to board *Carpathia*.

Four hours earlier, at 4.30 am, Captain Stanley Lord was awakened by chief officer George V. Stewart, then *Californian*'s officer of the watch. Going on deck, Lord saw with the morning's first light some clear water to the west, and at 5.15 he ordered the engines

Above left *Lifeboat 14, commanded by fifth officer Harold G. Lowe, approached* Carpathia's *side with collapsible D in tow. (Mr and Mrs George Fenwick.)*

Above right *Collapsible D approached* Carpathia's *gangway doors. (National Archives.)*

Below left *Photographed from* Carpathia's *deck by Mrs James Fenwick, one of her own passengers, the twin-peaked berg is described by surviving* Titanic *passengers and crew as the one with which their vessel collided. (Mr and Mrs George Fenwick.)*

Below right *Lifejackets lay abandoned in the lifeboat as survivors prepared to board* Carpathia. *(Mr and Mrs Arthur Dodge.)*

on standby. About this time the chief officer pointed out a four-masted steamer with a yellow funnel, bearing south-south-east from *Californian*. He expressed concern that the ship might be in distress, perhaps with a broken rudder, and said the second officer had told him the ship appeared to have fired several rockets during the early watch.

The captain had the telegraphist roused and ordered him to find out the vessel's name and whether she required assistance. Evans turned on his set and sent a 'CQ' — 'All stations, someone answer'. He was astonished to receive a response almost instantly from the German steamer *Frankfurt*, which advised him that during the night *Titanic* had sunk at 41.46N, 50.14W, a position Evans immediately took to Captain Lord on the bridge. Lord quickly worked out the location to be S 16 W, about 19½ miles from *Californian*'s estimated position. He immediately ordered *Californian* under way with the entire crew alerted. Thus, for the first time in seven hours, the *Californian*'s engines throbbed to life.

Following zigzag courses between south and south-west, *Californian* pushed through the ice at no more than six knots. Reaching open water at about 6.30, the ship proceeded at full speed — 70 revolutions, or about 13½ knots — southwards, down the icefield's western edge.

Around 7.30 *Mount Temple* was passed, stopped in the wirelessed position of the sinking. There was no sign of wreckage in this location. *Californian* continued south, soon passing a pink-funnelled, two-masted ship heading north — *Almerian*, a vessel lacking wireless. Soon *Californian* sighted *Carpathia* on the ice field's eastern side, abeam and to the south-south-east, and confirmed by wireless that she was picking up survivors. Lord altered course and sped through the ice, stopping alongside *Carpathia* around 8.30 am, their position approximately 41°33' N, 50°01' W.

After circling the area to ensure that there were no more survivors, Captain Rostron ordered *Carpathia* under way, leaving *Californian* to search for any further survivors clinging to rafts or wreckage.

Ruth Becker Blanchard recalls,

'When all the lifeboats were in and there was no hope of picking up any more persons, the *Carpathia* got ready to start for New York City at Monday, noon. That was the saddest time of all. That was the time when so many of the women who had been put into lifeboats by their husbands — and told they would meet each other later — realized that they would never see each other again. The women had been watching the lifeboats as they came in, looking for their husbands. They never saw them; they had gone down with the ship. We were so lucky because if my father had been along, he would have gone down with the ship, too.

'So, we started for New York City, going very slowly because we were still among the icebergs. . . The *Californian* came up alongside of the *Carpathia* and offered to take on survivors, but Captain Rostron refused.'

Rostron also arranged for a service of remembrance and thanksgiving to be held in the first class lounge. Following the service he ordered a count of surviving crew and passengers. *Carpathia*'s chief purser E. G. F. Brown, and second purser P. B. Barnett, prepared and checked the list of surviving passengers. *Titanic*'s second officer Lightoller

Left *At about 8.30 am* Californian *arrived at the spot where* Carpathia *was taking on the last* Titanic *survivors. It had taken the Leyland liner two full hours to avoid the huge ice-field separating her from the disaster site. This dramatic photograph was taken from* Carpathia's *deck by one of her passengers, Mabel Fenwick (Mr and Mrs George Fenwick.)*

Right *Aboard* Carpathia *as she sped toward New York,* Titanic's *survivors rested and recuperated from their dreadful ordeal.* (Harper's.)

prepared the deck and engine departments' survivor lists, while chief second class steward John Hardy assembled the victualling department list.

A check of the figures brought a chill of reality: of *Titanic*'s 2,228 crew and passengers, there were 705 living survivors aboard *Carpathia*.

It was as *Carpathia* left the disaster site that Rostron decided to return to New York. There was insufficient space to transport so many unexpected passengers. Nor were the galley's supplies adequate. The return journey began slowly — it took four full hours to skirt the immense ice pack.

By now survivors' lists were complete. After re-checking them carefully Rostron had them taken to the wireless shack. Telegraphist Harold Cottam had not slept for almost thirty hours. Besieged with requests for information, his temper and his ability to function were beginning to wear thin. To the operator of the Russian steamer *Birma*, in sight, close enough to receive some of the lists via small boat for wireless transmission to shore, Cottam inquired abruptly if *Birma* were a 'Marconi boat', that is, did it use Marconi apparatus? Receiving a negative response (*Birma* had a DeForrest installation), Cottam sputtered, 'Then shut up and stop jamming my signal'.

Competition was very keen among the fifteen or more wireless companies in 1912. Operators were instructed not to handle or relay messages involving other companies' traffic. Even now, close to total exhaustion, Cottam would not break the Marconi Company's strict rule.

Crowds filled lower Broadway seeking news of the disaster at White Star's New York offices (right). (Washington Evening Star.)

In Titanic*'s home port, hundreds crowded into Canute Road, the site of White Star's Southampton office, seeking word of her crew's fate. (Southern Newspapers plc.)*

To maintain communication between *Carpathia* and the outside world, Captain Rostron prevailed upon Harold Bride to join Cottam in the wireless room. Bride had to be carried from the dispensary, where he had been receiving treatment for severely frost-bitten feet. Cottam snatched a few hours' sleep while Bride continued transmitting. Both Cottam and Bride ignored all information requests from private and public sources. Even a personal request from American President William Howard Taft regarding his close friend Major Archibald Butt went unanswered.

One of the few land stations with apparatus powerful enough to receive *Carpathia*'s signals was on top of Wanamaker's Department Store in New York. Here for many exhausting hours its twenty-one-year-old operator David Sarnoff sat crouched over his receiver jotting down the names as he received them from the rescue ship and releasing them to the New York press for the world to read.

Interference from amateur and professional stations was so severe that the spellings of many names as received by Sarnoff did not resemble those of *Titanic*'s people. Only after a hasty and impassioned plea to President Taft himself were all wireless stations ordered to cease transmissions and 'give way' to traffic between MPA (*Carpathia*) and MHI (Wanamaker's). Even an attempt by John Jacob Astor's family to use the family yacht *Noma*'s wireless, MJS, in a private inquiry was rebuffed.

Finally a stronger link was established. At President Taft's order, the US Navy scout cruiser *Chester* was dispatched from Nantucket, Massachusetts, to accompany *Carpathia*

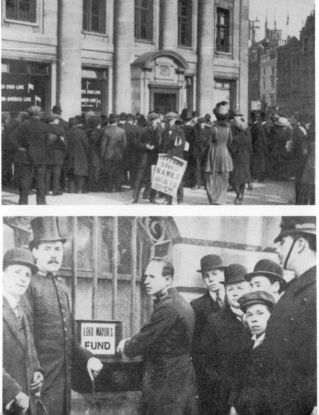

An anxious crowd jammed the pavement outside Oceanic House, White Star's London office. (Authors' collection.)

Collection boxes for the Lord Mayor's Titanic *Relief Fund were strategically placed throughout London. (*Daily Graphic.*)*

Above, E. H. Rothrock of the Chronicle, and, below, Charles Aleck, who murdered him causelessly. As a "joke" fellow workmen of Aleck, who could not read, showed him the glaring headlines of the Titanic disaster and told him he was the subject. So Aleck came to Spokane from a logging camp and killed the editor.

Titanic's loss resulted in a murder. Charles Aleck (bottom), an illiterate logger in the state of Washington, was shown the Spokane Chronicle's *screaming* Titanic *headlines, and told they pertained to him. Enraged, Aleck went to Spokane and killed the newspaper's editor, E. H. Rothrock (above.) (*Portland Journal.*)*

The rescue ship Carpathia *offloaded thirteen of* Titanic's *lifeboats upon her arrival at New York on the night of 18 April. (*Harper's.*)*

Crowds awaited the appearance of Titanic's *survivors at Pier 54's entrance. (*Illustrated London News.*)*

and to use its more powerful transmitter to augment *Carpathia*'s weaker signals. (Bride later complained about the *Chester* operator's competence.) But by 17 April, as *Carpathia* neared New York, most survivors' names were known.

Carpathia's voyage to New York had not been particularly pleasant, with severe thunderstorms and a dense fog putting everyone's nerves on edge. But the warm reception survivors received from *Carpathia*'s passengers and crew certainly helped. Said Ruth Blanchard,

> 'The *Carpathia* was on its way to Europe when it picked up our distress call and came to our rescue, so it was [partly] full of its own passengers. Therefore the 705 extra survivors had no place to sit except in the dining saloons and [on] the decks. The children sat on the floor. I remember we children ate sugar lumps off the dining room table. At night our family slept in the officers' quarters, which were in the bottom of the ship. I didn't like that at all. It scared me to be way down there.
>
> 'There was really nothing to do. Everybody just sat around talking, telling about their experience, and crying.

Above right and right *All that remained of the world's largest liner were the thirteen lifeboats moored at Pier 59. Pillaged by souvenir hunters, the boats are thought to have rotted away later at a Brooklyn, New York boatyard. (Authors' collection and* New York World.*)*

The *Carpathia* passengers were wonderful. They couldn't do enough for us.
One lady gave Mother a dress. We wore our coats over our night clothes.'

At New York elaborate preparations were made to receive survivors and expedite their arrival with minimal red tape. Even sacrosanct United States customs regulations were suspended. To spare survivors from a crush of reporters and well-intentioned curious, the public was barred from *Carpathia*'s pier and from two adjacent blocks.

While apparently the idea met with government approval, the Cunard Company forbade *Carpathia*'s boarding by reporters and families while she neared New York. Thus, as *Carpathia* reached the lower reaches of New York Harbour on the evening of 18 April, she was surrounded by a flotilla of yachts and small boats. Each bore shouting newspaper reporters who held up large cardboard banners asking questions (or making offers to pay for 'exclusives'). Frequent explosions of magnesium flares for photograph taking added to the confusion.

Carpathia soon outdistanced these boats, but as she slowed near Quarantine to take aboard the port doctor, several reporters who had bribed their way aboard the tender *Governor Flower* tried to clamber aboard, and had to be manhandled away by *Carpathia*'s third officer Rees.

As *Carpathia* continued up the harbour, she was buffeted by strong winds and heavy rains. Angry lightning flashes illuminated the eerie scene as she quickly passed the Battery at Manhattan's southern tip, where more than 10,000 had gathered to observe her arrival. Around 8.30 pm she approached her pier, number 54, at the foot of West Fourteenth Street. But she wheeled to port, then made a starboard circle in the Hudson River, finally coming to a stop near White Star piers 59 and 60, at the foot of West Nineteenth and West Twentieth Streets. Here *Titanic*'s lifeboats were lowered from *Carpathia*'s davits and decks. The Merritt and Chapman tug *Champion* stood by as seven were placed in the water and four were lowered to her deck. (Two boats remained overnight aboard *Carpathia*.) Then as *Champion* towed the boats to the bulkhead between piers 58 and 59, their attendant crews tied them up in the water.

Carpathia slowly retraced the last few hundred feet to her own pier where she tied up at 9.30 pm.

Welcomed by tears and hugs of joy the survivors stepped wearily down the gangway and headed towards the street. Many departed for hotels, some to their own homes, and more than forty by ambulance to city hospitals for treatment of various minor complaints.

The 174 third class survivors disembarked around 11 pm, long after the others had departed. Many had lost all in the disaster and were destitute. White Star provided temporary aid, with assistance from numerous municipal and private relief agencies.

In contrast, several first class survivors departed from New York aboard private trains. Mrs Charles M. Hays, widow of the Grand Trunk Railroad's president, boarded a special train at Grand Central Station, while the Thayers and Mrs George Widener each had private trains awaiting at Jersey City, New Jersey, for transport to their Philadelphia homes.

Unemployed and unpaid since Titanic*'s loss, the crew gathered on the steps of the Institute of the Seaman's Friend in New York. (Authors' collection.)*

The line separating rich and poor, which had become non-existent during the hours of tragedy and the tumultuous days which followed, again was drawn.

Twelve-year-old Ruth Becker, her mother, brother and sister were well cared for:

> 'Finally, Thursday night, three days after the *Carpathia* rescued us, we landed in New York Harbour in the pouring rain. Good friends met us there and took us to a hotel. The next day Mother went shopping with friends and bought us clothes to wear. Luckily she had saved some money which she had pinned on her clothing.
>
> 'The hotel made us honorary guests and would take nothing for food and lodging. Everybody was wonderful to us!
>
> 'When we boarded the train to go to Indiana, Mother took me aside and said, "Ruth, don't you dare tell anybody that we are survivors of the *Titanic* disaster". Mother was so inundated with reporters bothering her, and they made her very nervous. And, too, she was afraid the passengers on the train would question her. I assured her I wouldn't tell a soul. But, when we got on the train, we were showered with candy and cookies and gifts for my little brother and sister from the passengers. So our trip to Indiana was a pleasant one. We were glad to be on dry land again!'

In May 1912, Denver socialite Margaret Tobin ('Molly') Brown presented a silver loving cup from the grateful Titanic *survivors to* Carpathia's *Captain Arthur Rostron. (Library of Congress.)*

Conditions for some had begun to return to normal. For others, things would never again be the same. Events had already begun to alter many lives, and indeed would leave their mark on an era. From this time and for ever, the name of *Titanic* never would be forgotten.

Yet there had been a time when the name *Titanic* was unknown, a time when the men who designed and built her and the yard in which she was launched did not exist. But destiny's relentless, unalterable flow brought time, place and men together, and what had been unknown became a dream, and the dream became a reality. . .

THREE
A Burst of Cheering

The shipbuilding firm of Harland and Wolff is situated at Queen's Island in Belfast, Ireland, on the River Lagan. Its origins can be traced to 21 September 1858 when Edward James Harland purchased the yard for £5,000 from his employer, Robert Hickson. On 11 April 1861, Harland took on as his full partner Gustav Wolff, nephew of G.C. Schwabe whose financial assistance had permitted Harland to purchase the company. New Year's Day 1862 saw the establishment of the company's name, Harland and Wolff, under which it has continued ever since.

Joining the firm in 1862 as a fifteen-year-old apprentice draughtsman, William James Pirrie soon became head designer and in 1874 was admitted to the partnership. With Sir Edward Harland's death in 1896 and Gustav Wolff's retirement in 1906, Pirrie became the company's controlling chairman.

Under Pirrie's planning and direction the yard underwent modernisation during 1906-8. Two enlarged building slips, numbers two and three, were constructed in an area previously occupied by three slips. An immense gantry, designed by the shipyard and constructed by Sir William Arrol and Company, Ltd, Glasgow, was erected over the two new slipways and covered an area of 840 by 240 feet.

The construction of the two new slips followed an agreement between Pirrie and Joseph Bruce Ismay, chairman of the Oceanic Steam Navigation Company Ltd which owned and operated the ships of Britain's great White Star Line.

Since construction of the first *Oceanic* in 1870 Harland and Wolff had built ships for White Star. The freighters and great liners all bore the stamp and the integrity of builder and owner, and helped immeasurably to make the name White Star respected throughout the shipping world.

Before his death in 1899, White Star's founder and president Thomas Ismay had planned four large liners, to be constructed and operated for comfort rather than speed. His successor and eldest son Joseph Bruce Ismay carried on his illustrious father's traditions. With the successive appearances of *Celtic* (1901), *Cedric* (1903), *Baltic* (1904) and *Adriatic* (1907) the White Star Line appeared to own the most modern and luxurious fleet of North Atlantic liners.

The 20,904 ton *Celtic*, almost 681 feet long, was the first vessel to exceed the size of the *Great Eastern* (1860). But within a mere six years *Celtic* herself was surpassed by all

Left *Joseph Bruce Ismay (1862-1936)* (The Shipbuilder.)
Middle *William James Pirrie (1847-1924)* (The Shipbuilder.)
Right *Alexander Montgomery Carlisle (1854-1926)* (Illustrated London News.)

three of her own sisters, culminating in the 709 foot long, 25,541 ton *Adriatic*.

Even these liners, the 'Big Four', were dwarfed by the 1907 appearance of the great new Cunard Line ships *Lusitania* and *Mauretania*. Constructed in response to five large German vessels built between 1897 and 1907, and heavily subsidised by the British government, the 790 foot *Lusitania* and *Mauretania* featured innovative propulsion, the steam turbine, which proved immediately and immensely successful.

The White Star Line's management immediately saw the advantages of the steam turbine's power and economy. In 1909 the company completed two liners, *Megantic* and *Laurentic*, identical except for their engines: *Megantic* was fitted with conventional piston-based reciprocating engines while *Laurentic* had a combination of reciprocating and turbine engines. *Laurentic* proved to be far more economical to operate, so White Star managers decided to adopt combination engines for the much larger ships then being planned.

With completion of Cunard's *Lusitania* and *Mauretania*, White Star had an urgent need to match the level of service and facilities provided by its British rival.

In late 1907, during an after-dinner conversation with J. Bruce Ismay, Lord Pirrie proposed the concept of three huge liners — two to be built first, followed by a third. The vessels, each fifty per cent larger than the Cunarders, were to be in keeping with White Star tradition of 'comfort rather than speed', emphasizing great elegance within while providing safety for passengers and economy of operation.

The names of the three sister ships later were chosen to be *Olympic*, *Titanic* and *Gigantic*. Both the shipyard and White Star positively, even vehemently would deny the selection of *Gigantic* as the third ship's name. No official or written source for the name can be found. Yet, in newspaper reports following *Titanic*'s loss, the name appears again and

Plans for Titanic *and her sister ship* Olympic *were completed in the draughting room at Harland and Wolff's Queen's Island yard in Belfast, Ireland. (Harland and Wolff Ltd.)*

again in such prestigious publications as the *New York Times* and *Lloyd's List and Shipping Gazette*.

Nor was this the first time the name *Gigantic* had been selected for a White Star Line ship. The following news story, reproduced here in its entirety, appeared in the *New York Times* dated 17 September 1892:

> 'London, Sept. 16 — The White Star Company has commissioned the great Belfast shipbuilders Harland and Wolff to build an Atlantic steamer that will beat the record in size and speed.
>
> 'She has already been named *Gigantic,* and will be 700 feet long, 65 feet 7½ inches beam and 4,500 horsepower. It is calculated that she will steam 22 knots an hour, with a maximum speed of 27 knots. She will have three screws, two fitted like *Majestic*'s, and the third in the centre. She is to be ready for sea in March, 1894.'

This vessel was never built.

Following the disaster to *Titanic*, the third vessel's name was quickly and officially changed to *Britannic*, a name always regarded as 'lucky' for the White Star Line. She was the second of their liners to be so named.

Plans for the three giant new vessels were drawn up by a team of designers. Prominent among these was Alexander Carlisle, Lord Pirrie's brother-in-law, who was responsible for the ships' internal arrangements, their decorations and their life-saving appliances.

The basic design was presented to White Star management during a special trip which J. Bruce Ismay made to Belfast on 29 July 1908. He approved the design, and a letter of agreement was signed on 31 July. (These 'letters of agreement', one for each ship, were the only contract, *per se*, ever signed between White Star and Harland and Wolff. It was each company's understanding that all White Star vessels were to be built on a cost-plus basis with only the finest materials and workmanship used. All bills from the shipyard were paid promptly and without question upon presentation.)

During the summer and autumn of 1908, working plans were completed, special supplies and equipment were ordered. The keel for Harland and Wolff's four-hundredth commission — yard number 400, *Olympic* — was laid in slipway number two on 16 December 1908.

Now, Lord Pirrie's foresight in developing the shipyard, in constructing the special slipways, in building the huge gantry became evident. Just a bit more than three months later, on adjacent slip number three, the keel for yard number 401 — *Titanic* — was laid on 31 March 1909.

Yard number 401 also bore the builder's hull number of 390904 — a number whose appearance almost caused construction work to stop. Perhaps it was first seen by a member of the draughting department straightening his tie in a mirror, or possibly by a yard worker catching a glimpse of the number reflected in a rain puddle. But regardless of the origin, the numerals, if hastily written and then read as a mirror image, spelled out to some the ominous words, 'NO POPE'. And in the hearts of the pious, working-class Catholic employees in Belfast, there was deep indignation until a delegation of their men was assured by management representatives that it was all strictly coincidence, and that no malice had been intended. In spite of the assurance, and although work resumed, the builder's hull number — for many then, and many today — spelled doom for the vessel.

Work on the twin giants proceeded rapidly, so rapidly that a rumour began to spread among yard workers. It is likely that it began at the end of a work day when, with all else quiet throughout the yard, an inspector was inside the hull checking a riveting crew's output for the day, tapping with his hammer to test the soundness of the rivets.

And perhaps a worker, leaving the yard late, perhaps resentful at having been driven too hard that day by an ambitious foreman, experienced a flash of superstitious insight and imagined he was hearing the attempts of a worker trapped inside the hull to attract attention, to get out of his prison. . .

October, 1910: Olympic *(right) neared completion while work on* Titanic *(left) continued. (*Engineering.*)*

And so the rumour began that workers were trapped into the hull because of the speed with which they were being impelled. This, too, some thought, doomed the ship.

Titanic's construction safety record was better than most. Far fewer deaths occurred than the 'one for every £100,000 spent' which was the rule of thumb in shipyards of the period. Just two fatalities in the period from keel laying to launch can be confirmed.

As the twin hulls grew, so did the public's interest. The *Olympic*'s launch on 20 October 1910 was described in great detail in all the scientific and shipping journals, just as it was in the popular press. While the fitting out of *Olympic* proceeded, work on *Titanic*'s great hull continued. Through the winter and spring of 1911 most purveyors of shipbuilding supplies and equipment included in their advertisements, 'As supplied to the great new liners *Olympic* and *Titanic*'. As the date for *Titanic*'s launch drew near even manufacturers of consumer goods such as soap and beer exploited either the new vessel's name or the fact that their product was used aboard.

The launch day — 31 May 1911 — was clear and mild. From early morning onwards yard workers and their families, visitors and distinguished guests began to fill the shipyard. Stands for special guests and the press had been built near the spot where the immense bows towered towards the blue sky. Earlier in the morning the specially chartered boat

Above Titanic *is seen under the great Arrol Gantry just prior to launch. (Harland and Wolff plc.)*

Right *Spectators entered the shipyard to witness* Titanic*'s launch on 31 May 1911. (*Illustrated London News.*)*

Duke of Argyll had brought from Fleetwood, Lancashire, to Belfast a party of reporters and important guests, including John Pierpont Morgan, the American financier whose International Mercantile Marine controlled the White Star Line.

As the hour for launching approached every seat in the stands was filled, as were all vantage points near the yard and up and down the River Lagan. It was later estimated that more than 100,000 people were present to view the event.

Shortly before noon a red rocket was fired from the yard to indicate that launch was imminent. On top of the front of the gantry the American flag flew on one side, the British Union Jack on the other. At the centre fluttered a large red company pennant with its

Above *Leaving a remarkably small wake for so large a mass . . . (Harland and Wolff plc.)*

Left . . . Titanic *entered the water shortly after 12.15 pm. (Belfast Telegraph.)*

five-pointed white star. A row of signal flags below spelled out the word SUCCESS. From the hull's stern flew the red launch flag.

All was ready. At 12.13 pm a second rocket shot into the air. The roar of the crowd stilled to an expectant murmur. Pirrie gave a quiet order to the launch foreman. There was no ceremony, no formal naming of the vessel. (The absence of a christening, some later said, was another reason for the vessel's demise. In reality, it was merely a continuance of standard White Star Line policy. *None* of their ships was christened.)

The knocking loose of the last timber supports was followed by a general shout of 'There she goes!' A burst of cheering rent the air as *Titanic*, her passage eased by 22 tons of soap and tallow spread to a one-inch thickness on the ways, slid gently into the water. Reaching a speed of 12 knots, the hull was gently stopped in about its own length and held in place by special anchors embedded in the river bottom and connected by seven-inch steel wire hawsers to eye-plates riveted to the hull's plating.

Having viewed the floating hull — the largest movable object yet built — for some time, the crowds strolled back into Belfast's streets. The hull itself, after being detached from the restraining anchors, was towed to its berth by five Liverpool tugs.

Lord and Lady Pirrie entertained a group of distinguished guests at the Queen's Island yard. Luncheon was served and congratulations were extended on all sides. The press and other favoured guests were served luncheon at Belfast's Grand Central Hotel, after which they were addressed by Harland and Wolff and White Star representatives.

At about 4.30 that afternoon, *Olympic* departed from Belfast, accompanied out of the Lough by the company's new Cherbourg tenders *Nomadic* and *Traffic*. At the mouth of the Lough, the tenders turned south for a direct voyage to the French port. *Olympic*, carrying among others J. P. Morgan and J. Bruce Ismay, headed across the Irish Sea to

Shipyard workers grappled for the ends of the drag chains used to slow and stop Titanic *after her launch. (*Cork Examiner.*)*

Liverpool, her port of registry and White Star's headquarters city, where, at Ismay's express wish, she was to be opened for two days of visits by local citizens.

From all parts of the British Isles came supplies and equipment for *Titanic*: tools, steel for plating and rivets, plumbing supplies, generators and electrical fixtures; wood for decking and panelling; caulking and cement and rivers of paint. Arriving by ship, train and truck, the thousands of components converged at the Belfast shipyards of Harland and Wolff.

Irish workers fabricated these varied materials into the great ship's developing form. Though her owner was American and her nominal owner English, *Titanic* was an Irish ship, built with the care, skill and integrity of Irish workers and craftsmen, built (as history would demand) to endure, in form, the cruelest indignity a ship can suffer.

But this was in the unforeseeable, unpredictable future.

Through the summer and autumn of 1911, as *Titanic*'s fitting out proceeded, the graceful though massive hull took on the trim look of a great liner. Deckhouses and superstructure were completed, individual cabins' bulkheads were installed, swimming pool tiles were laid, air ducts and electrical cables were threaded through the complex structure.

On 18 September 1911 the date for *Titanic*'s maiden voyage was announced through the publication of the company's 1911/12 winter sailing list: her debut was scheduled for 20 March 1912. But two days later an unforeseen event forced White Star to change this date and, in so doing, they altered the course of history.

On 20 September 1911, while departing from Southampton on her fifth voyage to New York, *Titanic*'s sister ship *Olympic* was rammed by the Navy cruiser HMS *Hawke*. The collision apparently resulted from a misunderstanding of the two vessels' intended courses. But a then little known element also played a role in the accident, an element which — almost seven months later — would have a similar, nearly tragic bearing on *Titanic*'s maiden voyage departure: the attraction which the hull of a vessel under way in confined waters can have for another vessel's hull.

Left *Great public interest was generated by the new liner, as evidenced by newspaper advertisements.* (Belfast Telegraph.)

Right *During a late February crossing from New York,* Olympic *broke a propeller blade. Between 1 and 7 March she returned to Harland and Wolff for repair while completion of* Titanic *proceeded.* (Merseyside Maritime Museum.)

Though damage to both vessels was fairly severe there were no injuries to passengers or crew. *Olympic* was laid up for two weeks at Southampton while temporary patches — wood above the waterline, steel plates below — were installed to cover the gash in her starboard hull. Departing from Southampton on the morning of 4 October, *Olympic* returned to Harland and Wolff, which had the only dry dock large enough to accommodate her for repairs. She arrived in Belfast two days later.

To make room for the damaged liner, *Titanic* was removed on 4 October from the Thompson Graving Dock and tied up at the Alexandra Wharf. *Olympic's* dry docking on 6 October permitted an accurate estimate of the time needed for her repair. It was also decided that, as long as she was at the yard, it would be as good a time as any to make minor modifications to certain first class areas, based upon her 'in-service' performance.

Titanic's construction had to be slowed as workers were diverted to complete *Olympic's* repairs. In several days it became apparent to the White Star management that *Titanic* couldn't be completed and adequately tested to meet the announced 20 March maiden voyage date. On 10 October the company released a new date: Wednesday 10 April 1912.

Her repairs completed, *Olympic* left Belfast and resumed service on 30 November. *Titanic* was returned almost immediately to the Thompson Graving Dock and fitting out continued with fully staffed work crews.

By the end of January, her funnels now in position, *Titanic* had assumed a nearly-finished form. In early March *Olympic* returned to Belfast for replacement of a propeller damaged on 24 February during an eastbound crossing. She was at the Harland and Wolff yard from 1-7 March. Photographs of the two sister ships show *Titanic* with lifeboats in place but the forward part of her promenade deck not yet enclosed. The alteration that would for ever distinguish *Titanic* from her sister ship was completed at the very last moment.

Monday 1 April was crisp and cool. But a brisk north-west wind swept across the region.

The Titanic *left the shipyard and proceeded down the Victoria Channel on 2 April 1912. (Private Collection.)*

It would complicate trials by making *Titanic* difficult to manage in the narrow confines of the River Lagan. Trials were postponed until the following day, and 'black gang' members received an extra five shillings pay for the delay.

Tuesday 2 April was a fine, clear and calm day. In addition to the 78 stokers and trimmers, 41 officers and senior crewmen (engineers, cooks and stewards) were aboard. Bruce Ismay couldn't attend because of family obligations; the White Star Line was represented by

Under tug escort she entered Belfast Lough for her speed and manoeuvring trials. (Harland and Wolff Ltd.)

Harold Sanderson, a senior member of the company's board of directors. Illness prevented Lord Pirrie from attending; Harland and Wolff was represented by Thomas Andrews, Pirrie's nephew, a managing director of the shipyard, and by Edward Wilding, a marine architect, as well as a nine-member 'guarantee group'.

Those who hadn't slept on the ship came aboard at a very early hour. By 6 am, with tugs fast, *Titanic* moved slowly away from her dock, out of the shipyard and into the Victoria Channel which led to the Belfast Lough.

Crowds of spectators lined the channel's landward side as *Titanic*, gleaming in the rising sun, swept majestically past, under control of the straining tugs: *Hornby* on the starboard bow line, *Herald* out in front on the forward line; *Herculaneum* and *Huskisson* on the starboard and port lines, respectively.

There was little sound except the excited approval of the spectators and the chug of the tugs' engines. *Titanic*'s own engines were not yet operating, although billows of black smoke from her funnels showed that the engine room crew was busy getting up steam.

Through the Channel and into the Lough, *Titanic* glided slowly, silently into the open water, still propelled by the tugs. Several miles down the Lough, about two miles off the Irish town of Carrickfergus, the procession came to a standstill. The tugs cast off and returned to Belfast harbour as *Titanic* stood alone, poised for the start of her trials.

The blue and white signal flag for the letter 'A' ('I am undergoing sea trials') was run up the halyard. On the bridge Captain Edward J. Smith issued a brief order. Fourth officer Joseph Boxhall grasped the handles of the engine room telegraph and thrust them forward. From the engine room far below the jangle of the repeater's bell sounded across the still

Titanic's public rooms were her builder's pride. The à la carte *restaurant offered* de luxe *fare at an additional fee for first class passengers. (Ulster Folk and Transport Museum.)*

Above left *The second class smoking room was found aft on B deck. (*The Shipbuilder.*)*

Middle left *The third class dining room set new standards of comfort for those travelling in steerage.* (The Shipbuilder.*)*

Below left *The new liner's cabins reflected the owners' penchant for comfort. A* de luxe *cabin on B deck cost £300 ($1,500) for two passengers and their servant. (*The Shipbuilder.*)*

Above *The décor of second class cabins was considerably less elaborate. (Ulster Folk and Transport Museum.)*

water, breaking the early morning silence.

Titanic's engines had been turned by her builders and engineers on several occasions during fitting out. But they had never exerted any power, nor had they been used to move the vessel. Now, as steam was fed into the great triple-expansion engines and the centre turbine, *Titanic* moved for the first time under her own power. The smooth waters of the Lough parted before her as, slowly but steadily, the ship got under way, her wake an immense 'V' ever widening behind her.

Through the morning *Titanic* steamed through her trials: stopping, starting and stopping again; turning in various circles at various speeds; helm over, back, then over again in a serpentine course; several combinations of her three propellers involved in making speed and turning calculations. . .

The owners' and builders' engineers and representatives, the Board of Trade official and senior ship's officers all gathered for lunch in the first class dining room to compare notes and observations. First impressions were optimistic and enthusiastic. The ship was functioning well, even better than predicted.

After lunch the major stopping test was conducted, with the engines reversed while the ship travelled at high speed. At 20 knots, *Titanic* took a bit less than half-a-mile — about 850 yards — to come to a complete stop.

With crew and officers at their respective stations, *Titanic* headed for the mouth of the Lough and the open waters of the Irish Sea. Turning south, the vessel travelled a straight course for about two hours down, about 40 miles, and two hours back to the Lough's mouth, at an average 18-knot speed.

Entering the Lough *Titanic* sailed towards the setting sun and Belfast. Still some distance from the shipyard, she stopped at about 6 pm. One more test was conducted for the Board of Trade's representative, Mr Carruthers: dropping and raising the port and starboard anchors. Satisfied that the new liner met all British government requirements, Carruthers signed *Titanic*'s passenger certificate, 'good for one year from today 2.4.12'.

With Board of Trade certification at hand *Titanic* was handed over by her builder, represented by Thomas Andrews, to her owner, represented by Harold Sanderson. Yard workers who were not to accompany the vessel to Southampton were lightered ashore. Brought out from shore and taken aboard were fresh food supplies, some last-minute galley equipment and several special chairs for the first class reception room.

A few minutes after 8 pm, lights ablaze, *Titanic* turned and passed into the night, departing from Belfast for the last time. Down the Lough, again into the Irish Sea, heading for Southampton where she was due on the midnight tide on 3/4 April. Crew watches were set. There was little sleep for the shipyard representatives, who moved throughout the ship, examining, testing and adjusting. During this passage, under actual sea conditions, she briefly reached 23¼ knots, the highest speed she would ever attain.

On through the night and into the morning *Titanic* shaped her course: the Irish Sea, St George's Channel, the Cornish coast. Late morning and early afternoon: around Land's End and into the English Channel. Later afternoon and early evening: approaching the Isle of Wight as darkness began to fall. Into Spithead, past the Nab Light Vessel; more slowly, now, into Southampton Water where the pilot came aboard.

It was nearly midnight, the time of high tide, when *Titanic* approached the White Star Dock. Here she was met by five Red Funnel Line tugs: *Ajax, Hector, Vulcan, Neptune* and *Hercules*. The tugs assisted the immense ship as, engines stopped, she entered the turning circle at the river end of the dock area and swung around to enter the dock stern-first. (Her 10 April departure would coincide with the noon low tide; a more convenient port turn from the dock would be permitted by the 'bow outward' position, to say nothing of a more handsome public presentation.)

After her 570-mile journey *Titanic* was warped into her mooring at Berth 44.

From the Four Corners of the Compass

Preparations to receive and service the '*Olympic* class' of White Star liners had been completed on both sides of the Atlantic. The new tenders *Nomadic* and *Traffic* had been constructed at Harland and Wolff especially to serve the needs of *Olympic* and *Titanic* (and the forthcoming third sister ship) at the French port of Cherbourg.

At New York City, piers 60 and 61 of the Chelsea pier complex — between 14th and 23rd Streets along the Hudson River (or, as it was known locally, the North River) — had been extended and enlarged to accommodate the new vessels.

At Southampton, 78 miles south-west of London, the new White Star Dock had been constructed for the weekly service the line planned to establish with its three sister liners. (*Oceanic* of 1899 was to be the service's third ship until completion of *Gigantic*, planned for 1914.)

Fresh from her sea trials, it was to Southampton that *Titanic* came for provisioning, staffing and the boarding of her first passengers, transforming her into the floating city

*Southampton's new deep water mooring facility was named the White Star Dock in recognition of the company for whose ships it had been especially constructed. (*Railway Magazine.*)*

of her owners' proud dream.

Provisions. Staff. Passengers. No matter how beautiful a liner's interior, no matter how trim her lines or how smart her appearance, she is not *alive* until she has passengers aboard, a staff to attend them and food from her kitchens to feed them. Just as equipment and pieces of her fabric came to Belfast from the four corners of the United Kingdom for the new ship's construction, supplies and foodstuffs for her larders now came to Southampton from the four corners of the compass. . .

Titanic's 'shopping list' was as impressive as the ship herself:

Fresh meat	75,000 lb	Oranges	180 boxes (36,000)
Fresh fish	11,000 lb	Lemons	50 boxes (16,000)
Salt and dried fish	4,000 lb	Hothouse grapes	1,000 lb
Bacon and ham	7,500 lb	Fresh milk	1,500 gals
Poultry and game	25,000 lb	Fresh cream	1,200 qts
Fresh eggs	40,000	Condensed milk	600 gals
Sausages	2,500 lb	Fresh butter	6,000 lb
Sweetbreads	1,000	Grapefruit	50 boxes
Ice cream	1,750 qts	Lettuce	7,000 heads
Coffee	2,200 lb	Tomatoes	2¾ tons
Tea	800 lb	Fresh asparagus	800 bundles
Rice, dried beans, etc,	10,000 lb	Fresh green peas	2,250 lb
Sugar	10,000 lb	Onions	3,500 lb
Flour	200 barrels	Potatoes	40 tons
Cereals	10,000 lb	Jams and marmalade	1,120 lb

Good Friday, 5 April 1912, was the only day upon which Titanic *was 'dressed' in her flags. (Private collection.)*

The special rooms on *Titanic*'s orlop deck designed for storage of liquid refreshments were also fully stocked:

Beer and stout	20,000 bottles	Mineral waters	15,000 bottles
Wines	1,500 bottles	Spirits	850 bottles

Taken aboard at Southampton between 4 April and sailing day on 10 April were great quantities of glassware, cutlery, and tableware:

Breakfast cups	4,500	Salt shakers	2,000
Tea cups	3,000	Salad bowls	500
Coffee cups	1,500	Pudding dishes	1,200
Beef tea cups	3,000	Sugar basins	400
Cream jugs	1,000	Fruit dishes	400
Breakfast plates	2,500	Finger bowls	1,000
Dessert plates	2,000	Butter dishes	400
Soup plates	4,500	Vegetable dishes	400
Pie dishes	1,200	Entrée dishes	400
Beef tea dishes	3,000	Meat dishes	400
Cut tumblers	8,000	Dinner forks	8,000
Water bottles	2,500	Fruit forks	1,500
Crystal dishes	1,500	Fish forks	1,500
Celery glasses	300	Oyster forks	1,000
Flower vases	500	Butter knives	400
Ice cream plates	5,500	Sugar tongs	400
Dinner plates	12,000	Fruit knives	1,500
Coffee pots	1,200	Fish knives	1,500
Tea pots	1,200	Table and dessert knives	8,000
Breakfast saucers	4,500	Nut crackers	300
Tea saucers	3,000	Toast racks	400
Coffee saucers	1,500	Dinner spoons	5,000
Soufflé dishes	1,500	Dessert spoons	3,000
Wine glasses	2,000	Egg spoons	2,000
Champagne glasses	1,500	Tea spoons	6,000
Cocktail glasses	1,500	Salt spoons	1,500
Liquor glasses	1,200	Mustard spoons	1,500
Claret jugs	300	Grape scissors	100
	Asparagus tongs	400	

The foremast's shadow fell across the ship's bridge while she was moored at Southampton. (Illustrated London News.)

The ship's linen stores were no less extensive:

Aprons	4,000	Double sheets	3,000
Blankets	7,500	Pillow-slips	15,000
Table cloths	6,000	Table napkins	45,000
Glass cloths	2,000	Bath towels	7,500
Cooks' cloths	3,500	Fine towels	25,000
Counterpanes	3,000	Lavatory towels	8,000
Bed covers	3,600	Roller towels	3,500
Eiderdown quilts	800	Pantry towels	6,500
Single sheets	15,000	Miscellaneous items	40,000

A national coal strike which had lasted six bitter weeks was settled on 6 April, not soon enough for coal to be sent from pithead to Southampton for *Titanic*'s voyage. Coal from five IMM ships in port, and coal left over from fuelling *Olympic* (which had departed from Southampton only hours before *Titanic*'s 3 April midnight arrival), was taken on board. Some 4,427 tons were added to the 1,880 tons already in the bunkers. (The week in port alone consumed 415 tons for steam to operate cargo winches and to provide heat and light throughout the vessel.)

Titanic's officers had come aboard at Belfast before the sea trials, as had the engineering officers and many senior crew members, such as department chiefs. Also boarding at Belfast were the two Marconi wireless telegraphers, senior operator John Phillips and junior operator Harold Bride. During the trials and the voyage to Southampton they had been busy fine-tuning their powerful new radio equipment and transmitting and receiving many messages for the owners and builders. The wireless operators were actually employed by the Marconi Company, and not by White Star, yet they did sign the ship's articles, indicating that they were under Captain Smith's command.

The staff of the *à la carte* restaurant, a separate concession, were recruited from among employees of Luigi Gatti's two London restaurants, Gatti's Adelphi and Gatti's, Strand. While far from being White Star employees, they also signed the ship's articles and received from White Star the nominal wage of one shilling for the voyage.

Titanic's eight bandsmen were not White Star employees, nor did they sign the ship's articles. Their employer was a Liverpool firm of musical directors, Messrs Black, who supplied orchestras for the liners of several companies, including White Star. The musicians

Below left *Heavy hawsers linked* Titanic *to Southampton's Berth 44. (Bob Forrest Collection.)*
Below right *A rare postcard shows the liner's stern and the Blue Ensign. (Bob Forrest Collection.)*

"TITANIC"
TAKEN AT SOUTHAMPTON
APRIL 8TH 1912. TWO DAYS
BEFORE SAILING

PHOTO BY THOS. PEARSE
58 QUEEN SQ. BRISTOL

boarded at Southampton as second class passengers on ticket number 250654. They were quartered on E deck, near the stern on the starboard side, in an un-numbered cabin adjacent to E106.

As chief officer of *Olympic*, Henry T. Wilde was familiar with the structure and operation of the new class of vessels. To utilise his knowledge the company transferred him from *Olympic* to *Titanic* to serve only during her maiden voyage, since he was soon due for his own command. But his presence caused a realignment of *Titanic*'s senior officers: William M. Murdoch, the previous chief, was moved to first officer; former 'first' Charles H. Lightoller became second officer, a place held previously by David Blair. The remaining officers — Herbert J. Pitman (third), Joseph G. Boxhall (fourth), Harold G. Lowe (fifth) and James P. Moody (sixth) — were unaffected.

(It may be imagined that Blair, known to his friends as 'Davy,' departed from *Titanic* with considerable reluctance. There is no public record of his reaction following the ship's loss. His only public appearance during later White Star service is as navigator aboard *Oceanic* when, on 8 September 1914, she became a total loss through grounding off Foula Island in the Shetlands.)

A majority of the crew — seamen, stewards, stokers, trimmers, greasers and kitchen helps — were signed on during Saturday 6 April. The prolonged coal strike had caused great hardship among Southampton's working class. Now there was not only an employment opportunity, but it was one aboard the newest, largest White Star ship under the command of Edward J. Smith, well known and liked by the workers. Hiring halls were crowded and the several seamen's unions, only lately influential in the shipping world, were well represented among those employed.

Thought for many years to have signed aboard on this day was a greaser from Liverpool named Frank Tower. Subsequently nicknamed 'Lucky' or 'Lucks' Tower because of his alleged presence aboard *Empress of Ireland* and *Lusitania*, as well as *Titanic*, Tower's reputation (and that of his supporters) suffers a small blemish when one vainly searches for his name or any approximate spelling of it on *Titanic*'s official crew signing-on list.

(Two who did sign aboard on 6 April have associations almost beyond belief with all the *Olympic*-class vessels: both stewardess Violet Jessop and fireman John Priest were aboard *Olympic* in 1911 when she collided with the *Hawke*; each survived *Titanic*'s loss, and that of the third sister, *Britannic*, when that vessel was sunk in the Aegean Sea by enemy action in 1916. John Priest's remarkable saga continued with his survival of the war losses of *Alcantara* and *Donnegal*. Forced to retire from work at sea because no-one wished to sail with him, he died of pneumonia in 1935.)

Also signing the ship's articles as a fireman on 6 April was a man who produced the 'Certificate of Continuous Discharge' book bearing the name Thomas Hart, 51 College Street, Southampton. The man was placed on the 8-to-12 watch and was lost in the sinking. Hart's aged, grieving mother was officially notified by the company that her son was dead. She saw his name posted on the 'List of Lost' outside the company's Canute Road offices. But she received the shock of her life on 8 May, when her son entered their

Southampton home alive as ever. He sheepishly admitted, first to his mother and later to authorities, that he had lost his discharge book in a pub, while drunk. No, he hadn't any idea who might have found it or stolen it and used it. No, he had not boarded the *Titanic* himself. He had wandered about in confusion since the disaster, sleeping here and there, afraid to show himself or come home. Hart's story had to be believed, for there he was. But the authorities never were able to determine who had used Hart's book to sign aboard *Titanic* and who, in Hart's name, had been lost.

Supplies and cargo continued being taken aboard. Most crew had signed on. (A total of 908 in 'working capacities' were aboard when *Titanic* departed from Southampton; one was to desert at Queenstown.) By Wednesday 10 April, on schedule, *Titanic* stood ready to receive passengers.

It is well known that there were premonitions of disaster regarding *Titanic*: Morgan Robertson's prophetic 1898 novel *The Wreck of the Titan* is one of literature's most unbelievable coincidences. William T. Stead, a first class passenger on *Titanic*, had not only written of a liner sunk by ice, but in another story had told of passengers aboard a sinking vessel unable to be saved because there were insufficient lifeboats. An 1874 work by American poet Celia Thaxter likewise described the unalterable fate of a collision between a ship and an iceberg.

But no premonition or paranormal experience can match the truth, the number of passengers who, for various reasons, cancelled passage aboard the ill-fated liner: documentation exists for the cancellation of 55 bookings.

Henry Clay Frick, an American steel baron, booked a suite in February 1912 but cancelled it when Mrs Frick sprained her ankle during an excursion to Madeira. John Pierpont Morgan took over the booking but cancelled when his business interests lengthened his stay abroad. The same suite was then booked by another wealthy American, J. Horace Harding, who later cancelled and changed his passage to the *Mauretania*. (While no record exists of the suite in question, it may have been the one occupied by J. Bruce Ismay during the voyage. It was, after all, available.)

With his wife and daughter, Robert Bacon, the American ambassador to France, had booked passage aboard *Titanic* from Cherbourg. Their sailing, however, was postponed due to the delay in the arrival of his successor, Myron T. Henrick. But the Bacon family did enjoy maiden voyage excitement, re-scheduling their passage to the first trip of the *France* on 20 April.

Mr and Mrs George W. Vanderbilt had booked passage aboard *Titanic* but cancelled it at the request of Mr Vanderbilt's mother, Mrs Dressler, who had an aversion to all maiden voyages. ('So uncomfortable. So much can go wrong. . .') She had no actual premonition of disaster, but her reasoning was persuasive. Though their luggage had been sent aboard, the Vanderbilts cancelled their booking. Their servant, Frederick Wheeler (himself a second class passenger) stayed aboard to tend the luggage and was lost.

Most cancelled bookings were more prosaic. Mr and Mrs James V. O'Brien were delayed when a lawsuit they had begun in an Irish court took longer than expected. Several passengers didn't like their accommodation, while others couldn't obtain the accommodation they desired. The Reverend J. Stuart Holden, vicar of St Paul's, Portman Square, London, cancelled his passage on 9 April due to his wife's illness.

Indeed, there were premonitions: Mr and Mrs E. W. Bill of Philadelphia, staying at London's Hotel Cecil, were anxious to sail on *Titanic*. A day or two before sailing Mrs Bill had a dream in which the vessel was wrecked. They cancelled their passage and sailed on *Celtic* instead.

And so it went: for reasons of health, for business, for lack of suitable accommodation, upwards of 55 passengers altered their plans.

Even among those who did not cancel there were forebodings. Walter Harris, of Enfield, and Percy Thomas Oxhenham, of Ponder's End, had booked for New York aboard *Philadelphia*. That sailing was cancelled due to the coal strike and the men transferred to *Titanic*. Before sailing, Harris visited some friends, among whom was a young lady who practised palmistry. After examining Harris's hand she declined to say what she had read, remarking only that she did not like it. Harris's little son suddenly asked, 'Is Daddy going to be drowned?' (Harris was lost, Oxhenham saved.)

But 1,320 passengers did not cancel — passengers who became featured players in one of history's most dramatic disasters. Among them was eight-year-old Marshall Briles Drew, who recalled shortly before his passing in June 1986 the circumstances leading to his *Titanic* voyage:

> 'My Uncle Jim (James Vivian Drew) and Aunt Lulu and I went to Cornwall, England in the fall of 1911. My father and his brothers were Cornish. We went to Cornwall to visit with Grandma Drew and other relatives. The oddity here is that we crossed on the *Olympic*, sister ship to the *Titanic*.
>
> 'As we were returning anyway, I assume my Uncle Jim decided on the *Titanic*'s maiden voyage, with all the hoopla!'

For Marshall, his aunt and uncle, and for the others on board, the hoopla was to turn to horror in five days. . .

FIVE
Park Lane and Scotland Road

Titanic's officers and senior crew had been aboard during the ship's entire stay at Southampton, standing regular watches and overseeing the loading of supplies, stowage of cargo and final preparations for sailing. The general crew — engine room men, stewards, seamen and the like — were not due aboard until sailing day. The official signing-on list bore the notation, 'Date and hour at which he [each crew member] is to be on board: 6 am 10.4.12'.

Sailing day, 10 April 1912. The sun rose over Southampton at 5.18 am to a generally fair morning with north-west to west winds, fresh and sometimes gusty. Daylight's first hour saw *Titanic*'s crew streaming from all parts of Southampton, converging upon the dockyard gate. Showing their discharge books there and passing through, they proceeded towards Berth 44, where *Titanic* lay sparkling in the rising sun, her black-capped funnels glowing in the early-morning light.

Again showing their books at the gangway, the crew hurried aboard and were directed to their quarters by petty officers and assistant department heads. Their bunks were found on four decks:

Deck	Location	Number	Crew
D deck	forward, at bow	108	firemen
E deck	forward, at bow	72	trimmers
	port side, a bit aft	44	seamen
	port side, further aft	62	second class stewards
		106	saloon waiters
		24	bedroom stewards
			miscellaneous cooks and kitchen staff
	port side, just aft of amidships		entire *à la carte* restaurant staff
F deck	forward	53	firemen
	port side, amidships	42	third class stewards
	starboard, amidships		engineer officers
G deck	forward	15	leading firemen
		30	greasers

The balance of the crew, those who performed miscellaneous functions — printers, bell-boys, clothes pressers, Turkish bath and hospital attendants, masters-at-arms, lamp trimmers, post office workers — were scattered in many small enclaves throughout the ship, near the locations where they were to perform their duties. This was especially true of the first class stewards and stewardesses, whose tiny cabins holding two, three or four were wedged into odd corners among the wide corridors and spacious cabins of first class.

The crew were happy as they came aboard, laughing and calling to one another, shoving in a friendly way to be first along the deck, through corridors and into quarters. Many had not worked since the coal strike which had begun more than six weeks earlier. All were happy to be aboard a brand-new ship commanded by the well-known and paternal Captain E. J. Smith.

Also aboard at 6.30 am was Thomas Andrews of Harland and Wolff. During *Titanic*'s construction Andrews (Lord Pirrie's nephew) was a managing director and head of the draughting department. With the intimate knowledge of the ship he thus gained, and with Alexander Carlisle's 1911 departure, Andrews was aboard on this maiden voyage to represent the builders, to determine whether adjustments in the ship's structure or machinery were necessary, and to superintend the Harland and Wolff workers (the 'guarantee group') who would effect this work.

Andrews worked on board almost the entire time she lay at Southampton. His notes of suggestions for improvement filled many pages. These were not major adjustments; the ship certainly was soundly constructed and capable of fulfilling her function. Rather, Andrews' notes related to improvement of *details* whose modifications would set *Titanic* apart and create a new standard of excellence and luxury the entire world would envy.

Andrews occupied cabin A36, at the port side of the after first class entrance. This cabin had been installed almost as an afterthought. It did not appear on *Titanic*'s cabin plans dated as late as January 1912. The room was added during last-minute modifications which included the forward promenade deck's enclosure. Centrally located, it was an excellent spot from which Andrews might oversee 'his' ship.

Captain Edward John Smith, 'E. J.' as he was affectionately known among more than a generation of ocean travellers, came aboard *Titanic* on sailing day at about 7.30 am and prepared to meet and assist the various officials whose approval would permit the vessel to go to sea. E. J. had served his apprenticeship aboard the *Senator Weber*, an American-built sailing vessel owned by A. Gibson & Co of Liverpool. Joining the White Star Line in 1886 Smith served aboard the company's major vessels — freighters to Australia, liners to New York — and quickly assumed command. As the ships grew in size, so did the importance of Captain Smith's presence. He worked his way up through *Adriatic*, *Celtic* and *Coptic* (the latter for experience in the Australian route) and *Germanic*, among others. He was *Majestic*'s captain for nine years commencing in 1895, during which period he made two trooping voyages to South Africa during the Boer War. For this service he was awarded the Transport Medal. In addition he was an honorary commander of the Royal Naval Reserve and, as such, had been granted warrant number 690 allowing him to fly the Blue Ensign on any merchant vessels he commanded.

Captain Smith was regarded as a 'safe captain' and, for the period, he probably was. Yet he had been in command of *Germanic* when on 16 February 1899 she capsized at her New York pier from ice accumulations in her rigging and superstructure. And he had commanded *Olympic* when she had been damaged in collision with HMS *Hawke* in September 1911. Earlier, in June 1911, while manoeuvring *Olympic* into her New York pier, he had damaged a tugboat with the thrust from one of the liner's propellers. It seemed that Captain Smith — along with most contemporary liner captains — had much to learn about the displacement effects of so huge a hulk as the vessel he now commanded.

At age 62, Smith was close to retirement. Since *Baltic* of 1904 he had taken out the company's newest liners on their maiden voyages. After *Baltic* came *Adriatic* in 1907, then *Olympic* in 1911, and now *Titanic*. It was generally thought that he would retire from White Star service upon completion of *Titanic*'s first trip. But an article appearing on 19 April 1912 in the Halifax, Nova Scotia *Morning Chronicle* quoted White Star officials as announcing that he would have charge of *Titanic* until the company completed the larger and finer steamer then under construction. There is no further evidence to support this statement. Yet, *Gigantic* was expected to be ready for her own first voyage by 1915. By the time he was 65 Smith would not have been the oldest captain commanding a transatlantic liner. Perhaps he might have been considering staying on, at least for three more years. . .

At 8 am the Blue Ensign was hoisted at the stern and the crew, under direction of petty officers, began to assemble on deck for muster. The ship's articles — the 'sign on list' — for each department was distributed to respective department heads. Captain Benjamin Steele, White Star's marine superintendent, supervised the muster as each man was scrutinized by one of the ship's doctors. A company representative further examined each department's final rosters, then handed them to Captain Steele who, in turn, took them to Captain Smith for examination and approval.

Not appearing on the muster lists were the names of several groups of workers — not company employees, yet surely not passengers: the five postal workers (three American, two British); the eight members of the ship's orchestra (travelling as, though not accorded the courtesies due to, second class passengers); the nine-member Harland and Wolff 'guarantee group' (Thomas Andrews would make a total of ten). Three of the group, including Andrews, were booked in first class, the remaining seven in second class. . . A total of 22 names were not on the 'crew list' but, nevertheless, were gainfully employed aboard ship.

While the crew was being mustered, the Board of Trade's final inspection was conducted by its Southampton representative, Captain Maurice Clarke. His major concern appeared to be the lifeboats. He examined them carefully and observed the manning, lowering and raising of two boats, numbers 11 and 15 on the starboard side, under the supervision of fifth officer Harold G. Lowe and sixth officer James P. Moody. Satisfied that the boats were in proper working order and their crews proficient, Clarke repaired to the bridge.

There, with *Titanic*'s commander, he reviewed the ship's papers. He was handed the 'Report of Survey of an Immigrant Ship', the same sheet on which the Board's Belfast representative Francis Carruthers had certified *Titanic* seaworthy for one year from 2 April 1912. Clarke signed the report twice, indicating that he had observed a satisfactory boat drill and that *Titanic* carried 5,892 tons of coal, sufficient to take her to her intended destination, New York.

The final formality came and went as Captain Smith handed to White Star's marine superintendent Steele the 'Master's Report to Company': 'I herewith report this ship loaded and ready for sea. The engines and boilers are in good order for the voyage, and all charts and sailing directions up-to-date. Your obedient servant, Edward J. Smith'.

There were handshakes all around, offers of congratulation and 'good voyage' as the two officials left the bridge.

They were replaced almost immediately by Thomas Andrews and the ship's proud owner Joseph Bruce Ismay. White Star's president had motored with his family to Southampton from London the day before; they had stayed overnight at the South Western Hotel, overlooking the docks. Mrs Ismay and the children were not going on the voyage, so it was with special interest that they examined the ship's luxurious interior as Mr Ismay conducted them on a personal tour.

Leaving the family in care of a ship's petty officer, Ismay and Andrews ascended the steep steps to the bridge where they, too, offered congratulations to the ship's commander. Neither Ismay nor Andrews would appear again on the bridge until almost exactly 96 hours later. . .

The boat train from London bearing second and third class passengers had left Waterloo Station at 7.30 am, arriving at the dockside shortly after 9.30 am. Passengers detrained and immediately boarded *Titanic* through the second class entrances, aft on C deck, and the pair of third class entrances, one further aft on C deck, the other at the forward bulkhead of the forward well deck.

Many of the 497 third class passengers embarking at Southampton were Scandinavians. The White Star Line advertised extensively throughout Norway and Sweden, and employed a large network of ticketing agents throughout the region. White Star competed with the Cunard Line for southern European immigrants, particularly on routes between Trieste and Genoa and Boston and New York. But in 1912, White Star ships from Liverpool and Southampton carried many Scandinavians to the United States, most of whom booked third class passage 'aboard the first available ship'. And today, 10 April 1912, the first available ship was *Titanic*.

Anderson and Andersson; Asplund — Selma and Charles, with five children; Berglund and Berklund; Hagland, Hansen; Johnson and Johnsson; Alma Paulson and her four children (mother and all children lost); Anna and William Skoog with four children (all six lost); John Svensson and Servin Swensson (Servin would survive and reach his destination in far-off South Dakota). . .altogether, 150 adults and 30 children.

Scandinavians did not have the monopoly on large families. Of 183 British third class passengers, nineteen were members of two families: Fred and Augusta Goodwin and six children, including baby Sidney; and John and Annie Sage with their nine children. (All nineteen were lost.)

Also on board were Frank and Emily Goldsmith, with their son Frank J., on their way to Detroit, Michigan; Leah Aks, booked through to Norfolk, Virginia to join her husband; with Mrs Aks her ten-month-old son, Frank, better known as 'Filly.'

Third class cabins were located on D, E, F and G decks with entrances forward and aft. The only connection between forward and after sections was a wide corridor running almost the entire length of the ship on E deck's port side. Stewards' accommodation lined this corridor, called 'Park Lane' by the officers and 'Scotland Road' by the crew. There were no connecting fore-to-aft passageways for third class passengers on other decks.

Veitchi-covered stairways in third class entrances opened on to linoleum tiled, steel walled corridors. Third class cabins ranged from tiny two-berth rooms to six- and even eight-berth rooms. *Titanic* was not designed to carry large numbers of immigrants, and thus had just a single area of open berths, on F deck near number two hatch. Many liners of the period still maintained a number of these dormitory-like open spaces for immigrants' berths.

An arrangement not unique to White Star ships but incorporating dividers built to 'White Star design' was an area on G deck between numbers two and three hatches. This space was given over to portable rooms whose movable steel walls enclosed variable spaces according to the number of third class passengers on board. Except for these portable rooms, almost all third class staterooms were panelled in pine and had veitchi floor coverings, a far cry from the bare metal walls and floors of earlier (and some contemporary) liners.

Now, for the first time since the Harland and Wolff workers had departed, the third class areas were filled with people, the walls resounding to the bustle, joy and sorrow of departure. There was confusion, too, as passengers tried to locate their cabins and, even when correctly directed by harassed stewards, wandered aimlessly about.

The boarding of second class passengers was more sedate and better organized. Their cabins were centrally located aft on D, E and F decks; there were two almost-adjacent entrances. One was equipped with an elevator that ran from G deck to the boat deck. Corridors were carpeted in two-tone red or two-tone green, and the walls were wood-panelled.

Second class staterooms aboard *Titanic* rivalled first class accommodation aboard almost any other ship of the period. The well-lit two-, three- and four-berth cabins, many of them outside rooms open to the sea air, were panelled in white. Each room was tastefully fitted with mahogany furniture and comfortable upper and lower berths, with sofa beds providing the 'odd berth', as needed. Cabins had linoleum tile floors.

As passengers boarded and were directed to their cabins, second class corridors filled with people: eight-year-old Marshall Drew, travelling with his aunt and uncle, eagerly anticipating his second Atlantic crossing in less than a year. Young Marshall and his Uncle Jim were permitted to enter the first class areas while the ship was loading; after walking the upper decks they visited the gymnasium. Returning to their own quarters they stopped at the first class barber's shop, which doubled as the ship's souvenir and gift shop, where Uncle Jim bought Marshall a ribbon similar to those worn by sailors on their uniform caps: 'RMS Titanic', it proclaimed in gold threads.

Seven-year-old Eva Hart and her parents Benjamin and Esther were on their way to Winnipeg, Manitoba, where Mr Hart was to start a business. Eva and her father were seldom separated, and together they travelled all over the liner. Mrs Hart was uneasy about the sea voyage and very apprehensive of the 'unsinkable' label which had been given to the new liner by the press. Once in her cabin, she never left it except for meals, spending her time reading and knitting. During daylight hours she slept, for she felt that the source of her foreboding would become known at night and she wished to be awake and alert then.

A 'Mr Hoffman', a single gentleman travelling with two small children, seemed furtive and unwilling to mingle with other passengers; Mr William Harbeck was travelling with two superb motion picture cameras and 110,000 feet of exposed film, much of it relating to the *Titanic*. Mr Lawrence Beesley, a Dulwich College science master, busied himself by examining all accessible areas of the ship with an objective eye.

Time passed. 10.30. . .11 o'clock came and passed. There was scarcely an hour remaining before departure. Moments before 11.30 am the boat train arrived, bearing many of the 193 first class passengers boarding at Southampton. It had left London's Waterloo Station at 9.45.

Many 'glamorous' passengers would board later that day at Cherbourg. But the first class passengers boarding at Southampton were surely exciting enough. . .

Isidor Straus, American merchant prince, and his wife Ida (active in many charitable causes), with Mrs Straus's maid Ellen Bird and Mr Straus's valet John Farthing; the famous theatrical producer Henry B. Harris and his wife René; Col Archibald Gracie, historian, author of a book about the American Civil War, returning to his Washington home with notes about the War of 1812 that he had completed after researching in England . . .Mrs Ida Hippach of Chicago and her daughter Jean. (More than eight years earlier, on 30 December 1903, Mrs Hippach had lost two of her sons, Robert, age fourteen and John, age eight, in the fire which destroyed Chicago's Iroquois Theatre and claimed 602 lives.)

Perhaps the most famous (and certainly the richest) passenger aboard was Col John Jacob Astor (his military title stemming from his command during the Spanish-American War), aboard with his bride of exactly seven months, Madeleine Force Astor (her age nineteen, his 48). Col Astor's personal fortune was estimated at between £15,465,000 and £20,620,000 ($72 million to $100 million). The Astor entourage included Mr Astor's manservant Victor Robbins, Mrs Astor's maid Rosalie Bidois and, because Mrs Astor was 'in a delicate condition', a trained nurse, Miss Caroline Endres, a graduate of St Luke's Hospital School of Nursing, New York.

This tidy little group, almost an entity in itself, occupied the 'parlour suite' on C deck, amidships (C62). It consisted of a sitting room, two bedrooms, a private bath and toilet, and two wardrobe rooms for trunks. Miss Endres occupied her own cabin, C45, where she presumably was on 24-hour call to Mrs Astor's 'condition'.

The parlour suites occupied by Mr and Mrs Astor and, across the ship, by Mr and Mrs Straus (C55) were of 'period' design: C62 was in Louis XIV style, while C55 was in Regency style. The furniture was oak, the carpeting deep blue. One might think there could be nothing more elegant afloat: yet there was, and it was aboard the same ship.

The two 'promenade suites' on B deck, just aft of the forward first class entrance and designated B51 (starboard) and B52 (port) each contained not only the parlour suites' amenities, but also had its own private promenade deck, extending the entire length of the suite and open to the sea's air and light. For each suite, the occupant received at no additional cost an inside cabin for his or her servant(s) — B101 for suite B51, B102 for suite B52.

Also on B and C decks were cabins which could be interconnected to form suites of two, three or even more cabins. Luxuriously fitted in period design with panelled walls and the finest styles of oak or mahogany furniture, they surely were in keeping with White Star's well-known partiality for comfort.

Other first class cabins were situated forward and amidships on D deck, and amidship on E deck's starboard side. Even this 'secondary' accommodation was very comfortably,

As Titanic *moved out into Southampton's River Test, the displacement of water caused by her passing broke the hawsers of the* New York *(left). The American vessel's stern drifted towards* Titanic *as the tug* Vulcan *(centre) succeeded in preventing the impending collision. (L'Illustration.)*

Titanic *passed the bow of* Oceanic *moored at Berth 38, the collision with* New York *having been narrowly averted. (*Daily Graphic.*)*

Third class passengers lined the poop deck's rails as Titanic *moved down Southampton Water towards the English Channel. (*Daily Graphic.*)*

THE TITANIC'S PASSENGERS TAKING THEIR LAST LOOK AT HOME.

A photograph taken as the boat was leaving Southampton on April 10th, showing, on the deck, some of the passengers who are probably among the missing.

if not luxuriously, fitted and surpassed similar rooms on other transatlantic liners.

11.30. . .11.45 am. Departure time was near. Trinity House pilot George Bowyer was already aboard, as indicated by the red-and-white striped pilot flag flying from the halyard. As 12 noon approached the Blue Peter was run up the foremast, signifying 'Imminent Departure'. On the bridge Captain Smith gave a quiet order to the quartermaster on duty, who gently pulled downward on the whistle lanyard. The roar of *Titanic*'s triple-valved whistles reverberated through the cool Southampton air. . .a second time. . .then a third.

From their positions at docking stations — Wilde and Lightoller at the bow, Murdoch and Pitman at the stern — the ship's officers reported by telephone to the bridge, where fifth officer Lowe relayed their messages to Captain Smith and Pilot Bowyer.

'Tugs all fast,' came the report.

'Let go all lines,' was the command from the bridge.

The immense hawsers splashed into the water and were quickly drawn ashore by the pierhead gang under the dockmaster's direction. *Titanic* drifted gently from her dock.

Not yet under her own power, she was pushed, pulled and nudged out of the enclosed dock area by five straining tugs of Southampton's Red Funnel Line — *Ajax, Hector, Neptune, Hercules,* and *Vulcan* — the same tugs that had assisted her upon arrival from Belfast.

Having left the crew muster for some last-minute, land-side recreation, including visits to at least two pubs, eight members of *Titanic*'s 'black gang' sped down the pier at the mighty whistles' first blast. Only two of them managed to scramble aboard before the crew's gangway was raised. The remaining six, including three brothers named Slade, stokers Shaw and Holden, and trimmer Brewer, were left at the dockside, frustrated in their attempts to reboard the departing liner. However, the situation had been foreseen: a group of substitutes was on board, and as *Titanic* departed from the pier, an adequate number were immediately signed on to round out each watch's roster.

At the dock's entrance *Titanic* nosed into the newly dredged turning circle and was manoeuvred by the tugs into a position facing down the River Test. The tugs cast off. An order from the bridge preceded a clang from the engine room telegraph. The two mighty bronze wing propellers began to turn slowly. Against the incoming tide, *Titanic*'s bow knifed ahead, slowly at first, then faster as more power reached her propellers.

On her starboard side the turbulence caused by the huge vessel's forward passage swept harmlessly into the River Test. To port, however, the Test Docks' bulkheads impeded the dispersal of the turbulence. *Titanic*'s immense bulk made it impossible for the displaced water to find an outlet.

Tied up at Berth 38 were *Oceanic* and *New York*, still temporarily out of service after the coal strike. Moored in tandem, they faced downstream, with *New York* outboard. Water displaced by the passing *Titanic* caused *New York* to bob, first up, then down as *Titanic* passed. The motion put such a great strain on *New York*'s mooring lines that they snapped with loud reports. As *Titanic* moved past, her speed was increasing and she was drawing water behind her. *New York*'s stern, now loose, began to arc out towards *Titanic*, passing broadside to her.

The new liner passes a yacht moored off the Isle of Wight. (Peter Pearce.)

The alert Captain Gale of the tug *Vulcan* managed to get the second of two wire ropes aboard *New York*'s stern as the unmanned American liner veered to within four feet of striking *Titanic*'s own stern. On *Titanic*'s bridge, instinctive reactions of Captain Smith and Pilot Bowyer also prevented the collision. The order 'full astern' was given quickly. *Titanic*'s forward movement was checked and, as the reverse force took hold, the vessel moved very slowly backwards towards the mouth of White Star Dock. Her entire length moved past *New York*'s stern, still quite close but under the restraint of *Vulcan*'s line.

New York had now broken fully loose from her mooring. But with more tugs at the scene and with more lines aboard, the wayward liner now drifted around the head of the Test Docks, her forward movement finally ceasing. Additional lines were placed on *Oceanic*, so that when *Titanic* passed again there would not be a repetition.

Titanic's departure had been delayed more than an hour. An ill omen, some thought. An inauspicious start. Did the delay and the near-collision mean *Titanic* was ever to be a 'late' as well as an 'unlucky' ship? Time would tell, perhaps. . .

Through the ocean channel, into Southampton Water, past the Isle of Wight to starboard, and around Calshot Spit's intricate turn *Titanic* glided. Pilot Bowyer's experienced skill guided the liner safely to the Nab Light Vessel, where he disembarked. Wishing a good voyage to all and mentioning that he would see them in a fortnight or so, 'Uncle George' quickly descended the Jacob's ladder and nimbly stepped aboard the bobbing pilot boat.

Cherbourg, *Titanic*'s next port, now lay less than seventy miles away. Then it would be on to Queenstown for a brief, noon stop. The open sea would be next, for an uneventful and, hopefully, smooth crossing to an arrival on the morning of Wednesday, 17 April at White Star's Pier 60 in New York.

A three-day turn-around. A New York departure at noon on Saturday, 20 April. . .

The French tricolour fluttering from her forward mast, *Titanic* picked up speed as she headed southwards in the afternoon sun, into the open waters of the Channel.

SIX

Westwards to Destiny

Without exception the 142 first class, 30 second class and 102 third class passengers boarding *Titanic* at Cherbourg arrived on the *Train Transatlantique*. The train, which took a little more than six hours to make the trip from Paris, departed from the Gare St Lazare at 9.40 am, almost at the same time that the London & South Western Railway's boat train left Waterloo Station on its 100-minute trip from London to Southampton.

Cherbourg had been used by White Star as its continental port of call since 1907, when the company inaugurated its Southampton-New York service. Cherbourg had a splendid harbour enclosed by a long sea wall, but it did not have docking facilities for large ships. Visiting liners had to anchor offshore while passengers and mails were ferried out aboard tenders from the maritime land station.

Continental passengers arrived at Cherbourg's Gare Maritime *aboard the* Train Transatlantique *after a six-hour journey from Paris. (Authors' collection.)*

White Star's two Cherbourg tenders brought passengers from the station to Titanic, *anchored out in the roadstead.* Nomadic *(left) took the first and second class passengers while* Traffic *accommodated third class passengers and mail. (Authors' collection.)*

To provide this service, White Star had two tenders constructed at Harland and Wolff's Belfast yard. Completed in time to serve *Olympic* on her 1911 maiden voyage visit to Cherbourg, the two tenders *Nomadic* and *Traffic* were now to serve the same function for *Olympic*'s sister, *Titanic*, on her own maiden voyage.

The *Train Transatlantique* arrived at the trackside marine terminal on time. Embarkation was scheduled for just after 4 pm, but *Titanic*'s near collision at Southampton had delayed her Cherbourg arrival until after 6 pm. ('. . .Would the passengers be so kind as to be ready for embarkation at 1730 hours?') Fortunately the weather was good. Had it been cold or raining the passengers would have had to wait inside, on the two tenders' confining decks.

It was a most interesting group of passengers who milled about inside and around the tiny terminal. The 'season' was nearly over and in addition to the customary business travellers, many socially prominent passengers were on the Cherbourg manifest.

Mrs Charlotte Drake Cardeza and her son Thomas of Philadelphia were accompanied not only by Mr Cardeza's valet, Gustave Lesneur, and Mrs Cardeza's maid, Anna Ward, but also by fourteen trunks, four suitcases and three crates of baggage, on which Mrs Cardeza would later place a value of £36,567 2s ($177,352.75). The Cardezas were booked for suite B51, the three-room complex with its own promenade on B deck's port side for which, according to a White Star brochure, they paid $4,350 (almost £890).

The notables also included American mining magnate Benjamin Guggenheim and his valet, Victor Giglio. (Mr Guggenheim's chauffeur, Rene Pernot, was aboard, too, travelling separately on his own second class ticket.) And there were Sir Cosmo and Lady Duff-Gordon, with Lady Duff-Gordon's secretary, Miss Laura Francatelli. (Lady Duff-Gordon was the internationally known dress designer, 'Lucile'. For some reason she and her husband were booked under the names of 'Mr and Mrs Morgan' and they occupied separate cabins.)

Mrs James Joseph Brown, better known to her friends as 'Molly', had been on holiday in Egypt where she met the Astors; eager to make the transatlantic crossing with them, Molly was able to re-book her White Star reservation to the earlier ship — *Titanic*.

Among the second class passengers, a young man booked as 'Baron von Drachstedt' found his accommodation unacceptable. He paid for and was assigned a cabin in first class, D38. (Later, during a hearing in the United States, the 'Baron' was to confess to being plain Mr Alfred Nournay.)

Another second class passenger was Samuel Ward Stanton, the well-known American marine editor and illustrator. Stanton was returning from Grenada, in Spain, where he had been sketching the Alhambra for murals and other decorations he was commissioned to do for the Hudson River Day Line's new steamboat *Washington Irving*.

Third class passengers boarding at Cherbourg were Syrian, Croatian, Armenian and other Middle Eastern nationals who had been routed from eastern Mediterranean ports via Marseilles to Paris and, now, to Cherbourg. The 102 members of the group were tired from their long trips and confused by the strange tongue in which announcements were made. Boarding could not come too soon for them.

By 5.30 those not already waiting on the tenders were asked to board. The 172 first and second class passengers and their luggage filled less than a fifth of the space on *Nomadic*, while the mails and 102 third class passengers with their luggage filled scarcely a quarter of *Traffic*.

After the delay caused by the near collision at Southampton, *Titanic*'s commander had not tried to make up lost time during the Channel crossing. The colours of a beautiful sunset were beginning to fade into darkness as *Titanic* moved majestically but cautiously through the opening in the port's sea wall. It was 6.30 pm when the liner dropped her anchor at Cherbourg.

The two tenders fussed out to the immense ship's side. Fifteen first class and seven second class passengers prepared to disembark. (These 'cross-Channel' passengers had been transported for £1 10s (£1.50) first class and £1 second class; their names do not appear on any printed or official list, but are on *Titanic*'s ticketing manifest. Also carried were seven 'local' first class passengers to Queenstown, at a rate of £4 each.)

Mails were transferred, 274 passengers and their luggage were taken aboard, some freight — four cycles, eight cases, and a canary consigned to a Mr Meanwell — were taken off. Within ninety minutes the ship was ready for departure. For the second time that day the mighty voice of *Titanic* spoke. Three times the deeply pitched three-tone whistle

Lights aglow, Titanic *arrived at Cherbourg at 6.30 pm on 10 April.* (L'Illustration.)

resounded through the low hills around Cherbourg, announcing to all that the giant was now ready to depart.

At 8 pm, the tenders having left for shore, the powerful windlass gear whirred and strained, hauling in the clanking chain and its dripping anchor. By 8.10 pm, all secure, the liner made a tight turn using her wing propellers, and was under way.

Passing through the Grande Rade and leaving the winking lights of Cherbourg far behind, *Titanic* passed into open water. The pulse of her engines quickened as through the night she moved across the Channel, around England's south coast and into the lower reaches of St George's Channel and the Irish Sea.

Morning found *Titanic* approaching the Irish coast, a brilliant sunrise off her starboard quarter. During the trip up St George's Channel adjustments to the ship's compass were made, necessitating several wide, sweeping turns. But the main wake and course lay towards Queenstown. Passing the Daunt Light Vessel and pausing to pick up the pilot, *Titanic* continued to the harbour opening at Roche's Point, her sounding line in constant use. At 11.30 am the great anchor was again lowered and *Titanic* prepared to take aboard passengers and the Irish mails.

From the shore about two miles away chuffed the two side-wheel, black-funnelled tenders *America* and *Ireland*. When serving White Star liners, the tenders usually loaded from the White Star wharf, located between Scott's Quay and the railway station at the western end of town. But today the volume of mail and passengers was abnormally large. The tenders tied up at the pierhead adjacent to the railway station so that passengers and mails could be taken aboard directly from the train. The tenders took about half an hour to

Passengers boarded tenders Ireland *(centre) and* America *(foreground), moored at Queenstown's railway station. Because of her immense size,* Titanic *had to anchor some two miles from town off Roche's Point.* (Cork Examiner.)

make the trip from shore. Ferried out were 113 third class and seven second class passengers. A total of 1,385 mail sacks was also taken aboard.

Disembarking at Queenstown were the 'six adults in Mr Odell's party', among whom was Francis M. Browne, a Belvedere College teacher and a candidate for priesthood. He had accepted Mr Odell's invitation to travel aboard the new ship from Southampton to Queenstown. Now, as the 32-year-old teacher boarded the tender for shore, he clutched a packet of exposed photographic plates, pictures he had taken the previous day and earlier that morning around the liner's decks and public rooms.

Also debarking were a Mr E. Nichols, and one John Coffey. When the 24-year-old Coffey signed on *Titanic* as a fireman he gave his home address as 12 Sherbourne Terrace, Queenstown. It is possible that he signed on to get a free trip home. He came ashore hidden under some empty mail bags. (Coffey's next, and last, appearance is his signing aboard *Mauretania* as a fireman when that liner made her westbound call at Queenstown on Sunday, 14 April. How he explained the blank space in his seaman's book is not recorded.)

Coffey was not the only crew member with a fondness for Ireland's green hills. While passengers were boarding from the tenders, a member of *Titanic*'s 'black gang' — perhaps a stoker, perhaps a trimmer — took a brief, unauthorised break to climb the ladder inside the dummy fourth funnel. His blackened, soot-covered face peering down at the clean, breeze-swept decks from on high caused thrills of revulsion and even fear to run through the minds of some passengers and crew who glimpsed him. The face quickly withdrew,

Left *With all passengers and mail aboard, fourth officer Joseph Boxhall (centre) and second officer Charles Lightoller prepared to order the closing of the gangway door for the last time.* (Cork Examiner.)

Below *As the tenders returned to shore (with Titanic's fireman John Coffey and seven cross-channel passengers aboard) the liner stood poised for her Queenstown departure.* (Cork Examiner.)

yet the appearance of this infernal-looking fellow was sufficient to serve, many said, as an evil omen, a sign of impending doom. (Those who now laughed at the superstitious fears of their fellow passengers had good reason to recall their own derision 3½ days later.)

Embarking from the tenders through the second class entrance aft on E deck came the additional second and third class passengers. The latter were quickly conducted across the entrance lobby to two doors on the port side, which opened on to the corridors of their own accommodation. Second class passengers remained in their area.

Among the third class passengers were Daniel Buckley; Katie Gilnagh; Eddie Ryan; Nora O'Leary; John Kennedy; Mary and Kate Murphy; Margaret Rice and her five sons, Albert, George, Eric, Arthur and Eugene (mother and five sons. . .all would be lost); James Moran; Agnes, Alice and Bernard McCoy; Eugene Daly. . .

Accompanying the tenders out from land were several small boats with merchandise draped over their bows and sides — soft goods, mostly: tweeds and laces which could be effectively displayed in the minimal time available to set up shop. The enterprising merchants were pleased to come aboard, by way of the tenders' decks, and allow their goods to be examined more closely. From one of these 'bumboat' men, and on the merest whim, Col Astor purchased for his young wife a fine lace shawl, paying £165 (more than $800) for it.

Again departure time approached. Again *Titanic*'s powerful voice spoke three times and the echoes resounded from the hills around the harbour. The tenders headed back towards land, the merchants' small boats dispersed. The anchor came up, dripping. With the American flag now fluttering from the foremast, the company's red pennant with its white star at the mainmast's peak, and the Blue Ensign waving from the stern flagstaff, *Titanic* began her stately departure.

From a spot on the third class promenade deck, aft, passenger Eugene Daly sounded his own note of departure. Coming out on the tender he had played some lively airs on his bagpipes, taking the edge off the sorrow of parting. Now, however, he saluted the receding land with the mournful dirge, 'Erin's Lament'. It was a fitting and nostalgic farewell to the beautiful country which so many would never see again. The great bronze wing propellers began to revolve slowly, then faster as more steam was fed to the engines.

There was a brief slowing down to drop the pilot at the light vessel, then a broad turn to starboard. Down the Channel, ever faster now that the centre turbine was cut in. The low green hills of Ireland swept past, became a blue line on the horizon, then a thin black thread which vanished astern as *Titanic* reached the open sea's swells. Now, irrevocably, her course was westward to destiny. Her destination. . .disaster.

★ ★ ★

On the North Atlantic the winter of 1912 was the mildest in more than thirty years. It allowed immense fields of sheet and floe ice to break off and drift further south than was normal, into the east-west shipping lanes. But the winter had been severe enough to drive the Gulf Stream and its moderating temperatures southwards, where its warmer currents no longer melted the ice pouring down from the north.

With the sheet ice came huge bergs, immense chunks of ice and debris 'calved' from Greenland's awesome glaciers, floating in silent solitude as great, ghostly presences. Some bergs resembled mountain ranges or great buildings or palaces; others resembled full-rigged ships.

Fully four-fifths of an iceberg's mass lies below water. As portions of the submerged mass melt, the berg's centre of gravity shifts, eventually causing the entire berg to capsize and present a new surface to the air. When this occurs the water still in the upper portion of the berg makes its face dark and especially difficult to sight at night.

As the water drains out of the berg's top portion, it once again assumes its pure-white guise. But even this colour change does not make it safe to approach. For below the water's surface pinnacles of ice have now become rock-hard spurs that protrude from the berg's main body, extending outwards to trap the unwary vessel that approaches too closely.

As many ships (most without wireless) reached port following the *Titanic* disaster they reported having sighted or having actually been in ice during the week of 7 April. A plotting of the positions reported by these vessels shows an immense ice field extending from 46° N to 41°31′ N, and from 46°18′ W, to 50°40′ W, moving southwards and slightly westwards as the week passed.

After departing from Queenstown *Titanic* quickly entered the North Atlantic lane for westbound steam vessels. Commencing on 15 January 1899, an agreement among the major shipping companies set the route for the 'summer season' (from 15 January to 15 August) as follows:

> (Westbound): 'Steer from Fastnet or Bishop Rock, on the Great Circle course, but nothing South, to cross the meridian of 47° West in Latitude 42° North, thence by either rhumb line or Great Circle or even North of the Great Circle, if an easterly current is encountered, to a position South of Nantucket Light Vessel, thence to Fire Island Light Vessel, when bound for New York, or to Five Fathom Bank South Light Vessel, when bound for Philadelphia.'

One can tell at a glance that a course which takes a vessel to a position of 42° N, 47° W will place it almost in the middle of the ice reported between 7 and 12 April. Even with wireless reports available to him and to his company, Captain Smith did not, nor was he advised by his company to, alter *Titanic*'s course from the season's established westbound route.

Titanic surged steadily onwards.

12 noon Thursday (11 April) to 12 noon Friday (12 April)	386 miles logged
12 noon Friday (12 April) to 12 noon Saturday (13 April)	519 miles logged
12 noon Saturday (13 April) to 12 noon Sunday (14 April)	546 miles logged

During these days, too, many eastbound and westbound ships reported heavy ice conditions along the lanes. On the night of *Titanic*'s departure, the French Line's *Niagara* reported being stopped and damaged by ice at 44°07′ N, 50°40′ W. She requested assistance and *Carmania* left her own course to stand by until it was determined that aid was not actually required.

President Lincoln, Corsican, Montrose, Lackawanna, Saint Laurent. . .all stopped in or passing heavy ice on 11/12 April. . .

Avala, California, East Point, Manitou. All encountering ice on 12 April, ice which lay along the sea lane. . .

Borderer, Minnehaha, Hellig Olav. Involved with ice during 13 April. . .

14 April. . . *Trautenfels. Montcalm. Canada. Corinthian. Lindenfels. Memphian. Campanello* . . .All reporting ice which lay ahead, directly in *Titanic*'s intended course.

* * *

As *Titanic* sped westwards the days passed calmly for passengers and crew alike. For the former, there were no formal activities, no general parties or organized recreation. Passengers were left to their own devices. The crew kept regular watches, pleased to be working on a clean new ship.

Third class passengers were provided with a general room, aft in the poop, on C deck. The cheerful room was panelled and framed in pine with a white enamel finish. Tables and chairs were teak, as were the comfortable contoured benches which lined the room.

For the men there was a smoking room adjacent to, but separate from, the general room. It was panelled and framed in oak, with furniture similar to that in the general room. There was a bar next to the smoking room and yet another third class bar forward on D deck.

Second class public rooms were aft on B and C decks. In appearance and comfort they rivalled first class rooms aboard most liners of the period.

Titanic's second class smoking room (aft on B deck) was handsomely panelled in oak. The comfortable oak furniture was upholstered in dark green morocco leather. The second class library, one deck below, was panelled in sycamore. Its mahogany furniture was tapestry-covered, and its windows were hung with green silk draperies.

The large oak-panelled dining room on D deck contained mahogany tables and chairs, the latter covered in red leather. The floor was linoleum tile. The dining room could seat 394 passengers.

The difference in rates paid by second class and first class passengers reflected not only the size, furnishings and fittings of cabins and public rooms, but also the number of amenities offered to first class passengers. They included a gymnasium; a plunge bath; a Turkish bath with Moorish decor; a verandah and palm court; a smoking room and a lounge (high on A deck, with its raised roof); and a stylishly furnished reading and writing room. There were not just one, but three elevators to speed passengers from the spacious public rooms on A and B decks to their cabins, amidships on B, C and D decks. The immense first class dining saloon on D deck with its adjacent reception room was one of the largest apartments afloat: seats for 532 passengers were placed about the numerous small tables seating from two to eight people — a far cry from the long rows of single tables with their closely-adjacent, bolted down seats found aboard many liners.

Dining hours were one of the few scheduled events in shipboard routine: 8.30 to 10.30 am for breakfast, 1 to 2.30 pm for luncheon, 6 to 7.30 pm, perhaps a bit later, for dinner. The *à la carte* restaurant was located on B deck, just aft of the fourth funnel. Its staff, recruited from Luigi Gatti's two London restaurants, worked for the Gatti concession and not for the White Star Line. The restaurant, with its light fawn-coloured French walnut panelling and two-tone Dubarry rose carpeting, seated 137 diners at 49 tables. It was open from 8 am to 11 pm daily for first class passengers with special tastes.

One of the special amenities which second class passengers shared with first class was the fine ship's orchestra. Consisting of eight talented musicians recruited from other ships, British restaurants and music halls the ensemble was led by 33-year-old Wallace Hartley, himself an accomplished violinist who came to *Titanic*'s 'band' from the Cunarder *Mauretania*.

The orchestra was divided into two sections, and members played interchangeably in each: a blue-jacketed trio consisting of piano, violin and viola or cello played in the second class lounge and dining saloon; the others played in various first class rooms, often the reception room and the dining room. In addition to providing luncheon and dinner music, they formed 'strolling trios' in the palm court and offered recitals in the lounge, while dressed in white jackets and dark blue trousers. Each player was expected to know from memory the 352 songs in the White Star 'music book' and to recognize them 'by the number' when called for by their leader.

Somehow the time passed quickly. There never seemed to be enough time to fulfil goals set early in the day. By nightfall, as passengers deserted the public rooms and sought the comfort of their staterooms late in the evening, there still seemed to be things to do, things to think about. . .

High on the bridge second officer Lightoller was relieved at 10 pm by first officer Murdoch. Lightoller made the rounds of the ship before turning in to his cabin aft of the wheelhouse on the port side. Perhaps before falling asleep he reviewed in his mind the cargo, the contents of the holds whose loading he had supervised. Nothing of any great value: pharmaceuticals, botanicals, opium instead of gold in the specie room. (Smiling, perhaps) 'Spices instead of specie. . .'

In his office on C deck starboard of the first class forward entrance, purser Herbert W. McElroy checked the day's receipts from the bars and the Marconi room before placing them in his safe. He noted the special packages in the vault, given into his personal keeping, instead of being consigned to the cargo holds.

'Nothing special here,' he mused. He leafed through his own copy of the cargo manifest . . .'Nor here. Just routine express cargo. Certainly nothing that's heavily insured. No instructions for special handling, either. Well, one good thing. . .It won't take long to unload.' McElroy folded the manifest and placed it in the safe with the package list. He closed and locked the safe door. Securing the office, he crossed the first class forward entrance and went towards his unmarked cabin next door to C53.

In the controller's office just off the *à la carte* restaurant entrance, manager Luigi Gatti was also tallying the day's receipts. He briefly recalled his wife's premonition. She had not wanted her husband to make this trip and told him that she 'felt strange about it.' He had shrugged off her fears, telling her that nothing could happen to him, that he was an expert swimmer and could easily get to land. 'You worry too much', he told her. 'Didn't I get through the collision aboard the *Olympic* last year without a scratch?' Gatti stepped into the restaurant to dismiss the remaining staff for the night; among them were several of his cousins. He then descended to his C deck cabin, between those of chief steward Latimer and ship's assistant surgeon J. Edward Simpson.

In the first class dining saloon, a group of men had gathered earlier that evening for dinner. At the table was the English journalist and editor William Thomas Stead, going to America to address a peace conference at President William Howard Taft's request. Stead also was a believer in mysticism and spiritualism. He frequently consulted mediums and investigated psychic phenomena. (Today he would be called a 'ghost chaser'.)

In 1886 he had written a fictional article for the *Pall Mall Gazette* in which he described a ship's loss through collision with another ship. Great loss of life resulted because there were insufficient lifeboats to accommodate passengers and crew. In 1892 Stead wrote a lengthy article for the *Review of Reviews* entitled 'From the Old World to the New', depicting a journey from England to the United States. The voyage is made aboard the White Star liner *Majestic*. During the crossing the liner rescues survivors from a fictitious craft sunk after collision with ice. *Majestic* herself must steer south to avoid striking the ice-field. During the past several years, Stead repeatedly had been advised by mediums to avoid ocean travel. He himself had recently given a talk in which he described himself in a shipwreck, calling for help. Now, in the spring of 1912 he was making his own crossing 'from the old world to the new' aboard a White Star liner, captained by the man who had once been master of the *Majestic*.

During dinner on the second or third evening out, Stead regaled table companions with stories of travel and spiritualism. One of the party, Fred Seward, recalled Stead relating a story of an Egyptian mummy carrying a curse that brought sickness, death and destruction to its owners. (The mummy in question — actually an inner coffin cover for a priestess of Amen-Ra — was currently on exhibit at the British Museum in London.) The look of terror and anguish in the painted eyes of the cover's main figure caused many who saw it to believe the occupant had suffered a tormented life, and there were some who wished to try to exorcise the evil spirit captured in the mummy's soul.

That Stead's tale of the mummy's curse left a great impression is beyond doubt. Seward, in a 19 April interview with a *New York World* reporter, related the dinner party incident involving Stead's story. In the emotion, exaggeration and distortion that followed the disaster, this tale of the mummy's curse became that of a real mummy aboard *Titanic* — one whose powerful spell had actually caused the wreck.

(The 'mummy saga' allegedly continues with its wealthy owner, also aboard *Titanic*, paying an immense bribe to have the case placed in a lifeboat, from which — presumably upon payment of another immense bribe — it was taken aboard *Carpathia* and secretly landed at New York. Its presence in the wealthy American's collection caused such devastation that the decision was made to return it to England; the case was taken to Canada where, on 28 May 1914, it was placed aboard the *Empress of Ireland*. . .)

Neither administrators nor trustees of the British Museum are empowered to sell or trade items from its collection to private individuals, no matter how wealthy.

The entire tale is one of fabrication and hysteria caused by the disaster's deep emotional impact. But because the story is directly related to an authoritative journalist who was also a believer in spiritualism, it was given credibility from the start.

A mummy case in whose painted eyes there is a look of anguish still exists, still owned by the British Museum. Its number: 22542. . .

The *Titanic* night moved on. . .

In her cabin Esther Hart sat knitting, 'looking after the ship' as her husband and daughter slept soundly after a day of exploration together.

In cabin E101 Miss E. Celia Troutt (later, better known by her married name Edwina MacKenzie) chatted with her voyage room mates, Nora Keane and Susie Webber. Before retiring, Nora related a conversation she'd had earlier with Nellie Hocking from Cornwall. Nellie said that as night fell she had heard the sound of a cock crowing. Cornish folklore called this a sign of impending disaster. ('. . .Of course it's true. Listen! You can almost hear it yourselves!')

And well might the room mates and Nellie have heard a rooster crowing. Among the items in Mrs J. Stuart White's claim for loss of property were 'live poultry: roosters and hens from Chasse ile rage, Jardin d'Agriculture' valued at $205.87 (£42 4s, or £42.20).

In the third class butcher's care (as were all domestic pets, the remainder aboard *Titanic* being five passengers' dogs), the 'live poultry' would have been comfortably crated, carefully marked (to prevent their becoming a chicken stew) and kept near the dog kennels on F deck just aft of the third class galley. Naturally, the rooster(s) would have crowed, and it is quite likely that the sound might have travelled through the after area of the ship's lower decks. . .

On G deck, near the bow on the starboard side, the five postal clerks had finished their day's sorting. The three American clerks, William Logan Gwinn, John Starr March and Oscar Scott Woody, and the two British clerks, James Bertram Williamson and John Richard Jago Smith, had worked hard on the piles of mail and the huge, cloth sorting bags. The men were pleased to enjoy a relaxing evening in their salon, amidships on C deck, which they shared with the two Marconi operators.

Gwinn had been scheduled to 'work' the *Philadelphia* but when news of his wife's illness reached him he had requested and received assignment to *Titanic*'s earlier crossing. Woody was looking forward to his 44th birthday on Monday 15 April. Aware that he would be celebrating it away from his wife, his postal colleagues had planned a little party for him. . .

It was a routine night aboard *Titanic*, similar to those aboard all ocean liners. Soon the night would pass, dawn would come, a new day would follow, and then another routine night. . .

The dawn of 15 April 1912 was not to come for *Titanic*. In a cataclysmic encounter with one of nature's most awesome creations, the newest and largest of man-made objects was destroyed, sunk in a matter of two hours and forty minutes.

The grief and sorrow *Titanic*'s loss engendered has never fully disappeared: man's memory for grief is long. Immediately following the disaster, this mourning was most intense, for it was during these days that the bodies of the lost were recovered. And it soon became apparent that the vast majority of the victims never would be found. They would sleep for eternity in the sea which now claimed them as her own. . .

SEVEN
City of Sorrow

Within hours of *Titanic*'s loss, much of Canada had witnessed an eclipse of the sun, 'the greatest this country has seen in 53 years,' according to a Halifax, Nova Scotia newspaper. To some it seemed to be a celestial reflection upon the passing of a giant. Even as the *Carpathia* made her way to New York, the White Star Line had begun preparations with Halifax as the focal point. The arrangements there concerned *Titanic*'s passengers and crew, but the reunions that would result would be far less joyous than those at New York's Pier 54.

By 15 April, *Titanic*'s owners had arranged for an attempt to recover the tragedy's victims. A. G. Jones and Company, White Star's Halifax agents, chartered the Commercial Cable Company's cable ship *Mackay-Bennett* to search the Atlantic's wide waters. John Snow and Company Ltd, the province's largest undertaking firm, was asked to oversee funeral arrangements. More than forty members of the Funeral Directors' Association of the Maritime Provinces agreed to assist Snow's in preparing the recovered dead for burial.

By Wednesday, 17 April, the necessary supplies — tons of ice, embalmer's tools, and

Workmen loaded a hundred coffins on to the cable ship Mackay-Bennett, *first of four White Star-chartered ships to depart from Halifax in search of* Titanic's *victims. (*Philadelphia Inquirer.*)*

Tons of ice were also a requisite for Mackay-Bennett*'s grim voyage. (*Halifax Morning Chronicle.*)*

more than a hundred coffins — had been stowed aboard *Mackay-Bennett* at her Halifax pier. The all-volunteer crew, under Captain F. H. Lardner's command, would receive double wages for the unpleasant task they faced and the vessel left port at noon.

Most other ships were already giving the scene of *Titanic*'s loss a very wide berth. What captain wished to show his passengers a grim panorama of wreckage, ice and bodies buoyed by white lifejackets, giving the appearance of seagulls on the surface? 'It's a hoodoo area,' some captains said. 'Best to keep the living away from the dead.'

Other captains became censors. On board the Uranium Line's *Volturno* westbound from Rotterdam, Captain Nelson learned of the disaster from his wireless operator. Only these two men knew of it until the liner reached port, the captain deciding to withhold the terrible news even from his officers. (Eighteen months later, *Volturno* herself would be in the news with her destruction by fire.)

The primary reason for vessels to avoid the disaster area was more basic: the North Atlantic passenger steamship companies had already shifted the shipping lanes far to the south, belatedly reacting to the now-obvious dangers of ice. Nevertheless, several vessels were passing through the area where *Titanic* had gone down, and these ships' wireless reports now guided the *Mackay-Bennett* to the disaster site. The North German Lloyd liner *Rhein* reported bodies and wreckage in latitude 42.01 N, 49.13 W. The *Bremen* sent word that she had passed more than a hundred bodies at latitude 42.00 N, longitude 49.20 W.

One of *Bremen*'s first class passengers, Mrs Johanna Stunke, later told the press, 'We saw the body of one woman dressed only in her night dress, and clasping a baby to her breast. Close by was the body of another woman with her arms tightly clasped round a shaggy dog. . .We saw the bodies of three men in a group, all clinging to a chair. Floating by just beyond them were the bodies of a dozen men, all wearing lifebelts and clinging desperately together as though in their last struggle for life'. To the north was the glistening bulk of a low-lying iceberg. The ocean's surface was covered with deck chairs and other wreckage.

Mackay-Bennett arrived on the scene at 8 pm on Saturday 20 April and recovery operations began the following morning. The cable ship's boats were lowered, and 51 bodies were recovered despite heavy seas. As each body came aboard, a square of canvas with a stencilled number on it was attached. Valuables and personal property were placed in canvas bags bearing the same number. A full description of the victim, including hair colour, height, weight, age, birthmarks, scars and tattoos was recorded in a ledger on the corresponding page number, along with a complete inventory of jewellery, clothing and pocket contents. These details, it was hoped, would permit identifications to be made.

After almost a week in the sea, many of the bodies were in poor condition. Some showed signs of injuries sustained during the *Titanic*'s sinking. Others had been badly disfigured by sea life. At 8.15 pm a burial service was held on *Mackay-Bennett*'s forecastle deck as 24 bodies, wrapped in canvas weighted with iron grate bars, were recommitted to the sea. The remainder were embalmed for return to Halifax.

The fourth body found brought tears even to the eyes of *Mackay-Bennett*'s sea-hardened crew. It was that of a fair-haired boy about two years old, found amid a mass of wreckage. His entry in the ledger book was tragically brief: 'No identification. No effects'. The only child found during recovery operations, he, too, was prepared for entry into Halifax.

Names of the identified dead were sent ashore immediately via wireless. Others would have to await arrival of next-of-kin for identification.

Word of *Mackay-Bennett*'s mission spread, and a succession of ships began reporting bodies, icebergs and wreckage. The debris field was extensive: 'cabinet furniture, including chairs, writing desks, and stools' said one report; 'bedroom furniture and fittings, a considerable quantity of white woodwork and framing amongst which was a cabin door and its adjoining partitions', said another; 'an oak newel post; hats, polished and white painted woods, and a great square of probably forty feet dimensions which may have been part of the ill-fated steamer's deck' said a third.

By 23 April, *Mackay-Bennett* had eighty bodies on board, and had received additional supplies of canvas and burlap from the Allan liner *Sardinian* passing through the area. The following day found the ship in heavy seas and dense fog. Nevertheless, recovery operations began at 4.30 am and continued for fourteen hours. Eighty-seven additional victims were recovered, searched and tagged.

Aware that he and his ship soon would be overwhelmed through sheer numbers, Captain Lardner contacted White Star's New York office for assistance. On 21 April the company's Halifax agents chartered *Minia*, a cable ship owned by the Anglo-American Telegraph Company Ltd. A coffin shortage delayed her departure, but fully stocked with ice, grate bars, the coffins and embalming supplies, *Minia* left at midnight on 22 April to join the *Mackay-Bennett*. At 6.15 am on Friday 26 April the two cable ships began searching

The cable ship re-entered a silent Halifax Harbour with 190 Titanic *victims on board. Her flag flew at half mast. (*Harper's.*)*

together. Fourteen were found by noon, and these were placed aboard *Mackay-Bennett*, now filled to capacity. Her crew had found 306 bodies. Of these, 116 had been buried at sea. The cable ship now returned to Halifax with 190 victims on board, a hundred in all the available coffins, the rest in canvas.

Minia continued the search. Bad weather persisted, and after recovering seventeen more victims, Captain W. G. S. DeCarteret advised the White Star Line that the gales had swept the remaining bodies into the Gulf Stream. Fifteen of those found by *Minia* were returned to Halifax on 6 May, among them Charles M. Hays, president of the Grand Trunk Railway. As *Minia* left the area, yet a third recovery vessel, the Canadian Ministry of Marine and Fisheries' *Montmagny* was despatched on 3 May from Sorel, Quebec.

Upon *Mackay-Bennett*'s 30 April arrival at HM Naval Dockyard's north coaling wharf number four, the off-loading of the dead began under the watchful eyes of twenty sailors from the Canadian cruiser *Niobe*. The stout concrete walls surrounding the dockyard effectively shielded the proceedings from view. One enterprising journalist who tried to photograph the off-loading immediately had his camera confiscated under orders from Halifax's police chief.

The first to come ashore were the bodies that had been on the foredeck, mainly crew for whom there had been no embalming or other preparation. Then came the second and third class passengers, whose remains were swathed in canvas. Finally came the bodies of the first class passengers, all embalmed, most identified, and all in coffins on the stern.

As the last of the dead left the dockyard on horse-drawn hearses, Captain Lardner reluctantly gave in to reporters' requests for interviews. Squeezed into the captain's dayroom, the session went smoothly until a table collapsed and Captain Lardner ended the press conference. Yet another bad omen, some said.

First class passengers' remains were embalmed and placed in coffins stowed on Mackay-Bennett*'s stern.* (Harper's.)

At least one reporter decided to change it to a *Titanic*-related omen and wrote his report of the incident so that the table collapse occurred during a reception aboard the liner before her Southampton departure. 'This was much commented upon, the hope being expressed that no mishap would happen to the mammoth liner after she left port,' his account concluded. (Because much work remained to be done while *Titanic* was in port, no visitors — press included — had been permitted aboard at Southampton.)

Mackay-Bennett's arrival also set into motion the procedures designed by the Halifax authorities to ensure strict decorum, expedite the return of loved ones to next-of-kin, and comply fully with provincial and city regulations.

The Mayflower Curling Rink on Agricola Street was turned into a temporary morgue. Where curlers normally engaged in spirited contests, 67 canvas-enclosed cubicles were constructed, each large enough to enclose three coffins. After embalming behind partitions at the rink's western end, the coffins were brought to the cubicles where, under escort, family or friends could attempt identification. Only those bearing proof of their own identity and authority to act were admitted to the rink. The dead were to be kept at the rink for two weeks. Where faces were distinguishable, photographs of the deceased and additional descriptive details were taken to assist with future identification efforts.

The curling rink's second floor was converted into the coroner's headquarters, and the staff worked hard to process the required documents leading to the issuing of death certificates — small, crimson-coloured squares bearing the usual spaces for name, sex, age, date of birth, address, and occupation. For 'cause of death' it noted, 'accidental drowning, SS *Titanic*, at sea'. Valuables of the deceased were recorded and stored for safe keeping by the coroner's staff.

Body number 124, that of John Jacob Astor, was the first to be claimed and released

Left *Vincent Astor (right) arrived in Halifax to identify the body of his father, millionaire John Jacob Astor.* (Harper's.)

Below *In Halifax's non-sectarian Fairview Cemetery were buried 121* Titanic *victims. (Authors' collection.)*

from the rink. Identification had been relatively easy. His record noted that he wore a blue serge suit, a blue handkerchief with 'A.V.' on it, a belt with gold buckle, brown boots with red rubber soles, and a brown flannel shirt with 'J.J.A.' in its collar. Astor's effects included a gold watch, gold cuff links with diamonds, a diamond ring with three stones, £225 in English bank notes, $2,440 in American bank notes, £5 in gold, 7 shillings in

The gentle, curving rows of Titanic*'s dead filled a hillside at Fairview Cemetery. (Authors' collection.)*

silver, 50 francs, a gold pencil and a pocketbook.

Based upon relatives' instructions or, in some cases, upon outright guesswork about a victim's religion, those not claimed from the Mayflower Curling Rink were designated for interment at one of the city's three cemeteries — the non-sectarian Fairview Cemetery, the adjacent Baron de Hirsch Cemetery for the Jews, or the Mount Olivet Cemetery for the Catholics.

Mistakes did occur. Michel Navratil, a Catholic from France, had been travelling with his two sons aboard *Titanic* under the assumed surname of 'Hoffman'. Unclaimed by his estranged wife, his body was buried in the Jewish cemetery based on the assumed name.

Rabbi Jacob Walter decided unilaterally that ten bodies designated for interment at Fairview Cemetery actually belonged in the Baron de Hirsch Cemetery. As memorial services proceeded in the city, he had several workmen move the ten in question. White Star and provincial authorities discovered the unauthorized transfer, and upon further investigation, learned that four of the dead had been Catholics, while others were subjects of family instructions already in hand. As the *Halifax Evening News* pointed out, 'The coffins were somewhat damaged in the frequent changes to which they were subjected and it is said that someone will have to pay for new ones'. The identity of the party financially responsible is not recorded. The unauthorized transfers were cancelled.

Burials began on Friday 3 May at all three cemeteries. At Fairview, long trenches had been dug, and into these fifty coffins were placed. Graves were individually dug at Mount Olivet and Baron de Hirsch for fourteen additional burials that day. On Saturday, 4 May there was a single burial service, but it brought out all the concern and sympathy Halifax could muster. The little boy, unclaimed and seemingly forgotten, was to be laid to rest after all efforts at identification had failed.

His plight had deeply touched so many people that White Star and provincial authorities were swamped with offers to sponsor the little fellow's funeral. The decision was made

The Paulson family's sad story was recorded on their gravestone in Fairview Cemetery. Only Mrs Paulson was found and buried here. Gosta Leonard Paulson, it is now believed, was buried in an adjacent grave as 'the unknown child'. (Authors' collection.)

easier when Captain F. H. Lardner requested that he and the crew of the *Mackay-Bennett* — the people who had found the young one — be permitted to accept responsibility for the boy's burial. His request was granted.

St George's Anglican Church was filled to overflowing with flowers and mourners. Following the service, the boy's small white casket, covered with flowers, was carried from the church on the strong shoulders of six *Mackay-Bennett* crewmen and taken by hearse to Fairview Cemetery. There, on a hillside overlooking Fairview Cove, he was laid to rest with the others from *Titanic*. Captain Lardner and his crew paid for a granite marker, larger than most others, and bearing the inscription, 'Erected to the Memory of an Unknown Child Whose Remains Were Recovered after the Disaster to the Titanic, April 15, 1912'.

(The child has subsequently been identified tentatively as two-year-old Gosta Leonard Paulson, who boarded *Titanic* with his mother, sisters and brother at Southampton. Unknown to anyone at the time, his interment took place within just a few feet of the grave of his mother, Mrs Alma Paulson. His sisters and brother were never found.)

Meanwhile, *Montmagny*'s search had not been very successful. A dense fog still enveloped the area, and just four bodies were recovered. On Friday, 10 May, steerage passenger Harold Reynolds was found clinging to a life ring. Later that afternoon, a Syrian girl about fifteen years old was discovered and, ten minutes later, the body of C. Smith, a bedroom steward, was taken aboard. The next afternoon, an unidentified crewman was found and buried at sea 'with suitable services'. As the service proceeded, *Montmagny*'s bell began to peal eerily, seemingly of its own accord, though its ringing was actually caused by the stiff winds buffeting the ship.

Titanic's *violinist 'Jock' Hume was interred under a gravestone whose design was identical to most other victims' markers. (Authors' collection.)*

JOHN LAW HUME
DIED
APRIL 15, 1912.
193

On Monday, 13 May, *Montmagny* off-loaded the three coffins at Louisburg, Nova Scotia, for shipment by train to Halifax, and within 24 hours resumed her search. On her second trip only small pieces of wood were found, scattered to the east of the disaster site. Reaching the Gulf Stream as the eastern boundary of her search, she left the area late on Sunday, 19 May.

White Star made one last attempt to locate additional disaster victims. On 14 May the company chartered Bowring Brothers' *Algerine*, which departed from St John's, Newfoundland, one day later. During the voyage, a single body, that of saloon steward James McGrady, was recovered — the final victim to be found.

The six weeks of searching by four ships had yielded 328 dead, of which 119 had been buried at sea. Of the 209 returned to Halifax, 59 were claimed and shipped to other locations, while 150 were buried in the city's three cemeteries. Of all the 328 recovered dead, 128 remained unidentified.

Soon dark grey granite tombstones were installed over each victim's grave. Most were of identical size and shape. On their sloping top surfaces were engraved the names (if known), the words 'Died April 15, 1912' and the body numbers. In many cases the line reserved for the name was never filled in.

The transatlantic voyage that had begun in Southampton, Cherbourg or Queenstown with such excitement and anticipation had ended for these people, not in the United States, the land of dreams and hopes, of friends and family, but in the compassionate city of Halifax, in whose care their eternal rest would be assured.

For 1,314 others, the eternal sea would serve as well.

EIGHT

Questions and Answers . . . and Questions

That there had been a great disaster there was no doubt. That *someone* was responsible there also was no doubt. To establish responsibility — to say nothing of liability — there certainly was no doubt that official investigations were required.

Though *Titanic* was a British ship she was owned by an American trust. Though she sank in international waters, her destination was New York, and there her survivors had landed. In the United States Attorney General's opinion, jurisdiction did exist for a Congressional investigation with the right to subpoena British subjects to testify.

William Alden Smith, Republican from Michigan and a member of the Senate Committee on Commerce, was selected by his fellow senators to chair a sub-committee to investigate *Titanic*'s loss.

Smith hastily assembled a six-man committee whose members lacked comprehensive knowledge of ships or shipping. Smith himself asked most of the questions, sometimes piercingly correct and at other times almost bumbling. Smith opposed the Morgan interests which owned the International Mercantile Marine and, through it, controlled the White

Michigan's Senator William Alden Smith chaired the United States Senate's investigation into Titanic*'s loss. (Library of Congress.)*

Star Line, *Titanic*'s operators. Yet throughout the hearings he maintained an objectivity that caused many Americans to accept his results.

The Harter Act of 1898 permitted steamship disaster victims to sue ship owners if it were proved the vessel had been carelessly operated and that the owner or operators were aware of the negligence. Senator Smith hoped to prove negligence and thus provide his American constituency with such a right to sue *Titanic*'s owners and operators for damages. To this end he relentlessly questioned one witness after another in an exhausting marathon investigation.

Perhaps it was because Smith represented a mid-western state and not one from the

Above *Guglielmo Marconi, inventor of wireless, watched and listened intently as* Titanic's *junior wireless operator Harold Bride (right and below centre) testified in Washington.* (Philadelphia Inquirer.)

Right *White Star Line attorney Charles C. Burlingham (centre) escorted J. Bruce Ismay (right) to another day of intense questioning by Senator Smith's committee.* (Private collection.)

Titanic's crewmen gathered, awaiting their turns to testify before the Senate committee in Washington. (New York Times.)

more prestigious, industrial East. Perhaps it was the American press, taking its cue from its British colleagues, consciously or unconsciously questioning Smith's (and America's) *right* to investigate. Perhaps it was the grey, ubiquitous power of the Morgan interests, whose sworn enemy Smith was, initiating and then spreading rumours of his incompetency. Perhaps it was Smith himself — his direct, abrupt manner — and his haste in finding the truth of the matter. . .Whatever the cause, Senator Smith was quickly labelled a fool and his honest efforts mocked by the American press.

But Smith was no fool. He was an attorney, a builder and operator of railways, owner and publisher of a moderately sized newspaper. In addition he was a board member (and later chairman) of a company operating a fleet of Lake Michigan steamboats. Physically vigorous and mentally alert (his 53rd birthday occurred 12 May 1912, towards the hearings' conclusion), Smith's background and condition fully qualified him to serve as the *Titanic* disaster's chief investigator.

Smith presented a summary of the committee's activities to the United States Senate on 28 May 1912:

> 'We examined 82 witnesses upon various phases of this catastrophe, including 53 British subjects and 29 United States citizens. . ., 2 general officers of the International Mercantile Marine. . .all surviving officers, 4 in number. . .and

34 members of the crew. . .We took the testimony of 21 passengers of all classes and 23 other witnesses on subjects relating to our inquiry. We held our sessions in New York and Washington. . .'

Between 19 April and 25 May the hearings occupied seventeen days. Testimony and affidavits filled 1,145 pages. Senator Smith's report to the Senate was nineteen pages long, and exhibits filled another 44 pages. Altogether the investigation cost the American taxpayers $6,600 (approximately £1,360).

His report praised Captain Rostron and his heroic dash to save *Titanic*'s passengers; he dealt with shortcomings of wireless and telegraph services in the hours and days following the disaster. In the report's most strongly worded section he soundly condemned Captain Stanley Lord, *Californian*'s master, for his failure to respond to apparent distress signals from the sinking *Titanic*, thus establishing the tone for ensuing years of controversy.

Smith's recommendations were few but far-reaching.

Lifeboats: increased capacity, with a seat for each person aboard; adequate manning of lifeboats; lifeboat drill for crew and passengers.

Wireless: 24-hour manning of wireless equipment; action against amateur interference; reliable auxiliary power sources; maintenance of secrecy with all messages.

It would not take the United States Congress long to study and pass legislation embodying these recommendations.

On Saturday 20 May the Red Star liner *Lapland*, on which *Titanic*'s crew had stayed since their New York arrival, left for England. Just before the 10 am departure, Federal marshals served subpoenas on 29 *Titanic* crewmen to appear as witnesses before the Senate committee. *Lapland* had sailed down the North River, past the Statue of Liberty, and was well through Lower New York Bay before it was discovered that five crew with important testimony had left without being subpoenaed.

Senator Smith himself made a hasty telephone call to the Brooklyn Navy Yard, and a wireless message was sent to *Lapland* to stop and await a boarding party. A Federal marshal pursued the ship by tug. His mission was successful: five more were detained to testify.

Bruce Ismay had been anxious to return *Titanic*'s crew to England as soon as possible. In wireless messages sent as *Carpathia* steamed towards New York with *Titanic*'s survivors, Ismay requested that *Cedric*'s impending New York departure be held until surviving crew could be transferred to her. Ismay's intent was widely misinterpreted. Most thought he wished to shirk his and the company's responsibilities to ensure crew appearances at an American investigation.

In fact, the crew had no money and only the clothing on their backs. Their pay had stopped the moment *Titanic* sank, and Ismay knew well the heart-rending anguish the survivors' families were experiencing, awaiting the return of their loved ones. Thus, in the haste and emotion of the moment, Ismay acted in what he thought was the crew's best interests.

The ship's crew lined Lapland*'s rail as the liner approached the dock at Plymouth, England on 29 April 1912. (*Daily Sketch.*)

Philip A. S. Franklin, International Mercantile Marine's American vice-president, was aware of Senator Smith's pending investigation and dissuaded Ismay from expediting his own and the crew's return to England. To avoid adverse public opinion and complex legal problems, Ismay was forced to accept detention until released by Senator Smith and his committee.

Remaining at New York under subpoena were *Titanic*'s four officers and 34 'ordinary' crew. Aboard *Lapland* were 167 surviving crew, eagerly anticipating reunions with friends and families. After an uneventful crossing she arrived at Plymouth shortly after 7 am on Monday 29 April. After an agonising wait while mail and other passengers were off-loaded, *Titanic*'s surviving crew members were ferried ashore aboard the tender *Sir Richard Grenville*.

While the tender slowly steamed for the dock, members of the Board of Trade were already taking depositions and preparing affidavits. Not permitted to board the tender, some British Seafarers' Union members pulled alongside in a small boat and through a megaphone advised the crew to withhold statements until they could consult with their union representatives.

Titanic's crew believed they would be released upon landing. Not so. The Board of Trade wished to question each before releasing him to go home. Accordingly, bedding and provisioning has been provided in the dock's third class waiting room, sealed off behind a high iron fence. As friends and family vainly waited outside, the crew were interrogated inside by the board's representatives.

Public pressure and, perhaps, humanitarian instincts prevailed. Instead of holding the entire crew overnight, the Board released 85 seamen and firemen at about 1.30 pm after

A six-foot-high fence separated Titanic's *detained crew from relatives, the press and curiosity seekers at* Plymouth. (*Lloyd's* Deathless Story.)

extracting from each an oath that they would not talk to reporters. Leaving behind the cooks, stewardesses and stewards, the seamen and firemen departed from Plymouth for Southampton at about 6 pm aboard a special train.

At Southampton, even as the men were being released, an open-air service celebrating the crew's return was being held at the Marlands. Territorials, army and navy reserve men, and 50,000 civilians attended. Prayers of thanksgiving for the saved, of remembrance for the lost were offered — the same bittersweet mix of prayers said earlier on 19 April at St Paul's Cathedral in London, during the national mourning service.

As the shadows deepened and evening fell over Southampton hundreds of friends, family and well-wishers gathered at West Station. The train's arrival, 45 minutes ahead of schedule, was greeted with cheers and tears. Almost lost in the crush of the crowd, the surviving crewmen pushed through the pressing throng to join their waiting families. The station platform was illuminated frequently by photographers' flash powder.

Cheers died to a murmur as the crowd realised almost simultaneously that there were many crew absent. A brief moment of near silence gave way to mixed sobs and cheers as the men — families, wives, children, parents in tow — departed from the station and walked up the hill to the town and home. The train departed from West Station and moments later arrived at the Docks Station, where the frenzied scene of welcome was repeated.

The night of 29 April at Southampton was one of joy and gladness, of sorrow and recollection. Nowhere else in the world that night could be found within a single block joyous parties in parlour and pub celebrating a loved one's return, while several houses away widows and bereaved mothers mourned for loved ones who would never come home.

The second group of *Titanic* survivors, 86 stewards, stewardesses and kitchen staff, were

Above *Crewmen marched to a Southampton memorial service for their fallen comrades.* (Lloyd's Deathless Story.)

Left *A weary Bruce Ismay managed a tight smile but his wife beamed as the crowd welcomed them home upon their Liverpool arrival aboard* Adriatic. (Daily Sketch.)

released from Plymouth on Tuesday 30 April. Most boarded a special train for Southampton, where they arrived around 9 pm. The previous night's scenes were again repeated, this time with an air of finality. Except for the 34 crewmen and four officers being detained at Washington for the American inquiry, whose names were known, the crew members arriving this night at Southampton were the last. There would be no more. And a sense of loss, a great wave of shock and sorrow descended upon the city, as it had upon the world. . .

The remaining crew, including look-outs Lee and Fleet and quartermaster Hichens, arrived at Liverpool aboard White Star's *Celtic* on 6 May. Though on a smaller scale than that at Southampton, the celebration was no less joyous.

Bruce Ismay and *Titanic*'s four officers arrived at Liverpool on 11 May aboard *Adriatic*. Mrs Ismay had journeyed to Queenstown to board the liner on its inbound voyage, and as Bruce Ismay walked down the gangway, his wife followed, beaming, for in contrast to his treatment in America, Ismay was greeted with cheers from the large crowd gathered at the Liverpool landing stage. Mr and Mrs Ismay could scarcely press through the crowd to reach their motor car. Hands reached out to touch him amid cries of recognition. It was almost a hero's welcome. And as Ismay and his wife left the dock for Sandheys, their home just outside Liverpool, they appeared quite affected by the greeting.

Titanic's surviving officers were also greeted at the dock by relatives. But they were tight-lipped when it came to answering the press's questions. There were questions to be asked and answers that had to be given. Though nominally owned by an American corporation, *Titanic* was a British-registered ship, built under British standards, sailing under British regulations with a British crew. And it was to be a British commission whose Court of Inquiry would investigate the disaster and ensure that no other British ship would ever meet a similar fate. The American hearings had asked 'How?' The British investigation would ask 'Why?'

The British Board of Trade regulations defining ships' structure had last been revised in 1894 when the largest vessel afloat was the 12,950-ton Cunarder *Campania*. By 1911, *Titanic*'s completion saw size increased to more than 46,000 tons, with even larger British ships coming. With development of the 'super liners' (*Lusitania, Mauretania, Olympic* and *Titanic*) some political figures — among them the populist Horatio Bottomley — questioned the regulations, particularly regarding adequate lifeboat provision.

Indeed the Board had already considered this question. An advisory committee had met early in 1911 to discuss lifeboats and their relation to increased ship size and passenger-carrying capacities. While there were points remaining to be considered, the committee found no reasons for changing existing regulations, which were based upon cubic footage allotted to passenger accommodation. *Titanic*'s original designer, Alexander Carlisle, was so pleased that the committee would even *consider* the question of adequate lifeboats that he signed its final report with only the mildest protest.

Titanic's final plan included sixteen lifeboats. With seating capacity for 980 persons these met then-current regulations. Four Englehardt collapsible boats, with seating for

Left *John Charles Bigham, Lord Mersey, was appointed wreck commissioner for the Board of Trade's investigation into the* Titanic *disaster. He is shown here with his son, who was the commission's secretary. (*Daily Sketch.*)*

Below right *Sir Cosmo Duff-Gordon (to the left of model's fourth funnel) listened intently as George Symons described lifeboat 1's departure from* Titanic *with only twelve on board. (*Daily Mirror.*)*

196 persons, were added by *Titanic*'s designers and builders and represented capacity beyond the Board's requirements.

The 'Order for Formal Investigation' into *Titanic*'s loss, which granted authority to the inquiry under the Merchant Shipping Act of 1894, was initiated by the Board of Trade and signed on 30 April 1912. The Wreck Commissioner, Lord Mersey — John Charles Bigham, Baron Mersey of Toxteth (Lancashire) — had already received his authority through a 23 April warrant signed by the Right Honourable Robert Threshire, Earl Loreburn, Lord High Chancellor of Great Britain. The names of the five assessors to assist Lord Mersey were approved by the Home Secretary on 23 April.

A formidable battery of attorneys represented the hearing's many parties. Principal among them were Sir Rufus Isaacs, KC, the Attorney General, counsel to the Board; the Right Honourable Sir Robert Finlay, KC, MP, who headed the White Star Line's counsel; and Mr Thomas Scanlan (instructed by Mr Smith, solicitor), who represented the National Sailors' and Firemen's Union.

The Attorney General presented 26 questions to the commission to prove and for which they had to try and find answers. They concerned construction, navigation and ice warnings received by *Titanic*. A final question was added, though hearings were already under way, concerning the steamer *Californian*'s possible proximity to the sinking.

The hearings were conducted in the Scottish Drill Hall, near Buckingham Palace, where the acoustics were abominable. Sounds were subdued and dispersed as barely-heard, muffled echoes. The addition of sound reflectors to the front of the hall had little effect. Spectators, counsel and commissioners all strained to hear the testimonies.

Workmen prepared a large half-model of Titanic *to assist Lord Mersey and his assessors in visualizing the night's events.* (Daily Mirror.)

Among the hearings' highlights: early testimony of *Titanic*'s officers and crew describing the wreck's details; Captain Rostron's account of the rescue and Guglielmo Marconi's testimony regarding wireless's role in maritime safety; Captain Stanley Lord, *Californian*'s master, who appeared only as a witness, and who was accused of no wrongdoing during the hearings; Sir Cosmo Duff-Gordon and his wife (well-known as clothing designer 'Lucile') who satisfactorily explained to the commissioners how they managed to depart from the sinking *Titanic* in a lifeboat with a 35-person capacity but bearing only an even dozen; J. Bruce Ismay, who explained, again to the commissioners' satisfaction, that he had nothing to do with *Titanic*'s navigation, and that he left the sinking ship only after he saw no other passengers in the lifeboat's vicinity.

The hearings' concluding public sessions were occupied with technical testimony and evidence about *Titanic*'s construction and how it compared with other ships; about the Board of Trade's own lifeboat rules (and how the Board was diligently pursuing modification of them, an effort begun early in 1911, more than a year before. . .); about stopping and turning tests conducted with *Titanic*'s sister vessel *Olympic*. The testimony and public sessions ended on Friday 21 June. Eight days of summations and closing arguments followed. To determine guilt or innocence was not the commission's purpose. It was to establish right or wrong; to accept and praise right; to criticise wrong.

As the jury retired to consider its verdict, so did Mersey and his assessors then retire from public view to study the records of testimony, the exhibits and counsels' arguments. And a vast amount of information it was: the transcript of testimony alone consisted of 25,622 questions and answers, which filled 959 double-column folio-sized pages.

On 30 July the Mersey Commission presented its findings. Summarized in the briefest form they were:

That the collision of *Titanic* with the iceberg was due to the excessive speed at which the ship was navigated; that a proper watch was not kept, that the ship's boats were properly lowered but insufficiently manned; that the Leyland liner *Californian* might have reached *Titanic* if she had attempted to do so; that the track followed was reasonably safe with proper vigilance; and that there had been no discrimination against third class passengers in the saving of life.

The Commission exonerated J. Bruce Ismay and Sir Cosmo Duff-Gordon from allegations of improper conduct. The judgement recommended more watertight compartments on ocean-going ships, provision of lifeboat capacity for all aboard, and tighter rules regarding ships' look-outs.

Above *Look-out Archie Jewell ('X', top left) completed his testimony, and earned a rare 'thank-you' from Lord Mersey. The hearing room's seats were filled with press and spectators. (*Daily Mirror.*)*

Above left *Lord Mersey ('X') and his nautical assessors observed the lowering of an* Olympic *lifeboat at Southampton on 6 May. (*Daily Sketch.*)*

Right *Lady Lucile Duff-Gordon was one of just two passengers to testify at the British inquiry. (Her husband was the other.) (*Daily Graphic.*)*

Californian's Captain Stanley Lord (centre) arrived at the Board of Trade inquiry to give testimony as a witness. Only after he left the stand did the Board of Trade introduce a question implying allegations of Captain Lord's inaction while Titanic *sank.* (Daily Graphic.)

Lord Mersey praised the general conduct of passengers and crew, but regretted that none of the lifeboats — especially number 1 — had attempted to save the drowning. He highly praised *Carpathia*'s Captain Rostron. He was convinced that those aboard *Californian* had seen *Titanic*'s signals at a distance of from eight to ten miles and could have reached her without risk, thus saving the lives of many or all. In conclusion, Mersey severely blamed the Board of Trade for its failure to give earlier consideration to revising the Merchant Shipping Act of 1894.

Following the release of Mersey's findings, the London *Daily Telegraph* said this of the inquiry's report:

'It must be borne in mind that Lord Mersey's court was not in the ordinary sense a court of justice, and the results of its deliberations must not be regarded as a judgement. . .

'Technically speaking, the report is not the last word, but in practice it would probably be treated as though it were. It is difficult to suppose, for instance, that any court which had to inquire into the responsibility of the owners of the ship would disregard the expression of opinion by Lord Mersey and those who sat with him, and this particular point is one of vital importance. For if "fault or privity" can be brought home to the owners of *Titanic* the limitation of liability laid down by the Merchant Shipping Act — £15 per ton for loss of life, £8 per ton for loss or damage to goods — is wiped out and the damages of sufferers are left at large. . .'

According to the Merchant Shipping Act, *Titanic*'s owners were liable for freight losses of about £123,711 (about $600,000). Claims in American courts by relatives of those who

Right Californian's *apprentice James Gibson testified against his captain, Stanley Lord, at the British inquiry.* (Daily Graphic.)

Below *Lord Mersey (second from left, top row) and his assessors presided over the British Board of Trade's inquiry into* Titanic*'s loss, which received answers to more than 25,000 questions.* (Daily Graphic.)

lost their lives and businessmen who lost their goods ran into millions of dollars. The ship's owners, therefore, brought suit in American courts to limit liabilities under American law, which meant the value of thirteen recovered-but-used lifeboats, a small amount for pre-paid freight, and the value of passengers' tickets, or about £20,159 ($97,772.02) in all. It was against this amount that claims totalling £3,464,765 ($16,804,112) were filed.

The United States District Court, Southern District for the State of New York had jurisdiction over the case, mainly because *Titanic* had been sailing towards the Port of New York and because White Star's principal American office was there. Assigned to hear the case was District Court Judge Charles M. Hough. Early in the proceedings and in a separate decision, District Court Judge George C. Holt ruled that British law applied to the total claim limit.

*J. Bruce Ismay answered more than 800 questions during his testimony before Lord Mersey. (*Sphere.*)*

Between the action's initiation and the start of hearings (September 1912 to June 1915), Judge Hough withdrew due to ill health. Judge Julius M. Mayer thus heard the case.

The claimants wished to prove negligence; the White Star Line wished to limit its liability by proving that negligence had no part in the disaster. Meanwhile, in the case of *Ryan* v *Oceanic Steam Navigation Co Ltd,* a British jury found for the claimants. White Star appealed. But on 9 February 1914 Lord Justice Vaughan Williams dismissed the case and thus upheld negligence in *Titanic*'s navigation. Following this decision, many claimants withdrew their actions in the United States District Court and refiled them in British courts.

There were still a sufficient number of claimants — and claims — to make the American hearings more than mere formality. Harland and Wolff's naval architect Edward Wilding described in detail *Titanic*'s construction and safety features. Alexander Carlisle, in a sworn deposition made at London, reiterated his British inquiry testimony about *Titanic*'s inadequate lifeboat capacity. Far more passengers appeared and testified than had at either the Senate or Board of Trade investigations, including John B. Thayer, Karl Behr, W. J. Mellor, Mrs Jacques Futrelle. . .

Claims had been filed for loss of life and property. The largest for loss of life — $1,000,000 (£206,185) — was filed by the widow of New York theatrical producer Henry B. Harris. Mrs Charlotte Cardeza, wife of a Philadelphia, Pennsylvania millionaire, submitted the

S.S.s "OLYMPIC" AND "TITANIC," BUILDING BY MESSRS. HARLAND & WOLFF, LTD. BELFAST, FOR
THE WHITE STAR LINE.
EACH VESSEL FITTED WITH THE NEW WELIN DOUBLE-ACTING DAVITS.
HANDLING IN ALL 32 LIFEBOATS

largest claim for lost property — $177,352.74 ($36,567). The government of the United States filed one of the smaller claims: $41.04 (£8 10s 5d) for lost registered mail.

The diversity of property claims reflected the variety of passengers aboard *Titanic*. Among the hundreds of claims for lost clothing, jewellery and personal items were the following:

Eugene Daly	Set of bagpipes	$50.00
Emilio Portaluppi	Picture of Garibaldi, 'signed by him and presented by him to my grandfather'	$3,000.00

Above *It was shown at the New York limitation of liability hearings that even while* Titanic *and* Olympic *were under construction, White Star had considered equipping the two ships with 32 lifeboats each, more than enough to have saved everyone on board* Titanic. *(National Archives.)*

Right *At the limitation of liability hearings in New York, Mrs Charlotte Drake Cardeza filed a fourteen-page, $177,352.75 (£36,567) claim against the White Star Line for loss of her personal property.* (Philadelphia Inquirer.)

Among the evidence presented at the hearings was Titanic's *freight list, showing money White Star had received for carriage of cargo aboard the lost liner. (National Archives.)*

William Carter	One Renault 35 hp automobile	$5,000.00
Ella Holmes White	Roosters and hens from Chasse ile rage Jardin d'Agriculture [total, 4 fowl]	$207.87
Edwina Troutt	Marmalade machine	8s 5d
Hokan Björnström-Steffanson	Oil painting by Blondel, 4×8feet, 'La Circasienne Au Bain'	$100,000.00
Stuart Collett	Hand-written college lecture notes, two year course	$50.00
Hersh L. Siebald	Seven parcels of parchment of the Hebrew Holy Scrolls [Torah]	$250.00
Margaret Brown	Three crates of ancient models for Denver Museum	$500.00
Annie May Stengel	Copy of *Science and Health*	$5.00
Robert W. Daniel	Champion French bulldog, named Gamin de Pycombe	$750.00

The total for all claims, £3,464,765 ($16,804,112) had to be divided pro rata among all claimants. By December 1915 barristers on both sides reached a tentative settlement. On 28 July 1916, more than four years after the disaster, Judge Mayer signed the decree ending all *Titanic* lawsuits. The amount distributed among the claimants was £136,701 ($663,000).

Thus were responsibilities investigated and assigned. Some who were responsible bore no blame; others were assigned blame not rightfully theirs. Liabilities were set, many believed, far below their actual value. But the law, in all its infallible majesty, had spoken. Only time's passing would bring questions for which no answers had been provided, and answers whose questions had yet to be asked. . .

NINE

With Time's Passing

There is perhaps no more fitting conclusion to any *Titanic* story than to look both backwards and forwards. Backwards to a very brief consideration of three lives touched by their *Titanic* associations. Forwards to the discovery of *Titanic*'s broken wreck and what this discovery means to the ship and its memory, as well as to those who would exploit the wreck for their own selfish ends.

Joseph Groves Boxhall was born in Hull, Yorkshire, on 23 March 1884. He died on 25 April 1967. Prior to his joining *Titanic* at Belfast as her fourth officer, Boxhall had been thirteen years at sea. He served his apprenticeship with William Thomas, Liverpool and later served as an officer with the Wilson Line of Hull. Passing for his master's certificate at Hull in 1907, he joined the White Star Line and had served for five years prior to joining *Titanic*. He had by that time gained his extra master's certificate.

Following the *Titanic*, Boxhall served briefly as fourth officer aboard *Adriatic*. He was a sub-lieutenant in the Royal Naval Reserve and shortly before the outbreak of World War 1 was commissioned in a battleship for a year's training. When the war began he remained for a time with this ship, HMS *Commonwealth*, and was then sent to Gibraltar where he commanded a torpedo boat. He became a staff member of Gibraltar's commanding admiral, and remained at that post until the end of the war.

Returning to White Star, Boxhall continued to serve until well after that line's 1934 merger with Cunard. He served as first officer aboard several Cunard liners, including *Berengaria* and *Aquitania*, and eventually became chief officer aboard *Ausonia*, *Scythia* and *Antonia*. Of all the junior officers aboard *Titanic*, Boxhall stayed longest at sea, retiring due to ill health in 1940.

He maintained an interest in the sea and in *Titanic*, although he never participated actively in any public discussions of the disaster. While he did not encourage debate concerning his role that night, he was not reluctant to declare that he was always certain the position he calculated for *Titanic* was correct and there could be no reason for him to change his view.

When Walter Lord's book *A Night to Remember* was made into a film Commander Boxhall came out of semi-retirement to assist in the production as joint technical adviser with Commodore Harry Grattidge. He found it '. . .very interesting to see myself as I was 46 years ago'. It was Commander Boxhall's wish that, upon his death, he be cremated

Commander Joseph Groves Boxhall on the occasion of his serving as technical adviser in the 1958 film A Night to Remember. *(Courtesy of William MacQuitty.)*

and his ashes scattered at the site of *Titanic*'s loss.

The following extract is from the log of the Cunard motor vessel *Scotia*:

'MV *Scotia*, New York to Southampton, June 12, 1967, at 0938, Lat 41°46' N, Long 50°14' W, the cremated remains of the late commander J. G. Boxhall were scattered on the sea during a brief ceremony.'

Yet another to be touched very profoundly by the *Titanic* was Joseph Bruce Ismay. Born at Enfield House, Great Crosby on 12 December 1862, he was the eldest son of Thomas Henry Ismay and the former Margaret Bruce. Thomas Ismay had begun the White Star Line, officially known as the Oceanic Steam Navigation Company Limited, in 1867. It was managed by his own firm of Ismay, Imrie and Company, and upon his death on 23 November 1899 its control passed to thirty-six year old Bruce Ismay.

On 1 January 1900 Bruce Ismay took on as partner Harold Arthur Sanderson, an old friend who had been the company's general manager for the past five years. Under Bruce Ismay's leadership, with Sanderson's support and assistance, the White Star Line flourished. Plans were made to enter the Australian and New Zealand trades with several new steamships. Construction also began on three large liners to complement the 21,000-ton *Celtic*. (Launched on 4 April 1901 *Celtic* was Thomas Ismay's last ship and the first to exceed *Great Eastern* in tonnage. She was the first of the 'Big Four' liners — *Cedric, Baltic* and *Adriatic* were the other three.)

Ismay also presided over White Star's sale to the American-controlled International Mercantile Marine. This great combine was formed in 1893 from the American, Red Star and Inman Lines and through recent purchases or control of the Atlantic Transport, Dominion and Leyland lines. Reaching an 'understanding' with the major German Atlantic shipping companies, the combine dominated the North Atlantic freight and passenger trades.

(Resisting Morgan's offers, the Cunard Line had remained British. For their loyalty — and to preserve British interests in liners which might serve as transports and armed merchant cruisers in war time — the British government extended low-interest loans to Cunard, enabling them to build *Lusitania* and *Mauretania*, the largest and fastest liners of the day.)

Perhaps fear of this government-subsidized competition caused White Star shareholders to accept the Morgan offer. The sale, for more than £10,000,000, was readily accepted by shareholders, though personally painful for the Ismay family. In essence, White Star became an American-owned company on 1 January 1904. At Morgan's request, J. Bruce Ismay assumed the chairmanship of International Mercantile Marine, which he effectively managed along with his own company's operations.

White Star's fortunes were never better. During the next eight years many new freighters and liners were completed. An expanded New Zealand and Australian service was established. And to the already popular and profitable 'Big Four' were added the great *Olympic* and *Titanic*, with a third sister, *Gigantic*, well advanced in her planning.

With the company's success thus assured, Ismay wished to retire as IMM chairman to devote more time to his own company and to personal pursuits. In an Autumn 1911 exchange of letters, Bruce Ismay and Harold Sanderson reached an understanding that Ismay was to retire at the end of 1912 and that Sanderson would head IMM.

This proposal was acceptable to the combine's American interests, though there was some bickering about the actual date. Ismay himself had some second thoughts, particularly about the season in which his departure would occur. But finally a letter dated 26 February 1912 was sent to J. P. Morgan and Company at New York, citing 30 June 1913 as the date of Ismay's retirement and Sanderson's succession as chairman.

In April 1912 Ismay's presence aboard *Titanic* was twofold: to observe the liner on her maiden voyage and also to visit IMM's main American office in New York to discuss details of his forthcoming retirement. His 1.40 am departure from the sinking *Titanic* was fully vindicated by the British inquiry. It was established beyond doubt that there were no women or children — indeed, no other passengers — in the vicinity of the boat as it was being lowered. As Lord Mersey stated:

> 'The attack on Mr Ismay resolved itself into the suggestion that, occupying the position of managing director of the steamship company, some moral duty was imposed upon him to wait on board until the vessel foundered. I do not agree. Mr Ismay, after rendering assistance to many passengers, found "C" collapsible, the last boat on the starboard side, actually being lowered. No other people were there at the time. There was room for him and he jumped in. Had he not jumped in he would merely have added one more life, namely his own, to the number of those lost.'

Certain segments of the American press maligned Ismay. In a horrendous display of irresponsible journalism, one New York newspaper displayed his photograph surrounded by small pictures of women whose husbands had been lost. The picture's caption read, 'J. Brute Ismay'.

The British press was more kind. Several witnesses to Ismay's behaviour during the sinking testified on his behalf during the American inquiry. Their evidence was generally acceptable to the British public. To many, he had acted heroically during the liner's evacuation. When he returned to England aboard *Adriatic* on 11 May 1912, a large crowd of well-wishers cheered his arrival at Liverpool.

The British inquiry found him personally clear of fault. Yet he was never really happy again. Each anniversary, particularly, caused him great sorrow and self-recrimination. He was especially troubled by survivors' accounts, many over-dramatized to the point of untruth, which appeared continually in newspapers. His family was supportive, but his wife Florence would not allow the subject to be discussed or even mentioned. Bruce Ismay lived the rest of his life haunted by his own feelings of guilt.

He had wished to remain as White Star's chairman following his resignation from IMM, but the combine's American interests blocked his wish. However, he did remain a member of IMM's British committee until he resigned from even this post in 1916.

After leaving International Mercantile Marine and White Star, Ismay continued to serve actively as a board member with numerous companies, particularly the London & North Western Railway. When that firm became part of the London, Midland and Scottish Railway, Bruce Ismay was asked repeatedly to be the new system's chairman. But he always refused, never again wishing to be in a position of public prominence.

Following World War I he sold Sandheys, his country home near Liverpool, but still spent time each week in that city attending company board meetings. During the 1920's he spent much leisure time as his Irish estate, The Lodge, at Costelloe, County Galway, on Ireland's west coast.

While he withdrew from his active role in business, Bruce Ismay did not become reclusive. He enjoyed walking in London's parks and attending concerts. His house at 15 Hill Street, Berkeley Square, became a meeting place for friends and family at small dinner parties. Until his eyesight began to fail, he spent several successive seasons at a rented lodge near Gleneagles, in Scotland, where he engaged in his two favourite sports of shooting and fishing.

His own children — Margaret, Tom, George and Evelyn — were married now. There were grandchildren to brighten summer holidays. When The Lodge at Costelloe was gutted by a mysterious fire one winter, Ismay had the house rebuilt and took a lively interest in its redecoration.

In 1934 Bruce Ismay retired from active business life. The shipping company his father had founded, and whose fortunes he, himself, had helped to ensure, had merged with its great rival, the Cunard Line. Within two years, all but two of the ships bearing White Star's black-topped buff funnels had gone to the scrapyard, judged superfluous by the new management.

Late in 1936 a circulatory illness forced the amputation of Bruce Ismay's right leg. He was confined to a wheelchair, and could walk only with the aid of crutches. He was able to spend the summer of 1937 at a house in the country, returning to his Hill Street home in early autumn. Far to the north, the great *Olympic*, upon which he had lavished so many hours and so many hopes, was towed to Inverkeithing, Scotland, for final demolition. On 14 October 1937 he suffered a severe stroke and died three days later. His cremated remains were buried in Putney Vale Cemetery, near London.

Stanley Lord was born at Bolton, Greater Manchester on 13 September 1877. Of all the figures in *Titanic*'s story, perhaps none is so tragic as that of the master of the Leyland steamship *Californian*. As alleged by the Mersey commission, Captain Lord was aware — or should have been — of *Titanic*'s plight, but did nothing to save her passengers and crew, though his vessel was in a position to do so.

During the Board of Trade hearings, Captain Lord had appeared solely as a witness. He was not indicted (rightly or wrongly) for his role, and therefore was unable to appear officially and publicly in his own defence. The press, in accepting Lord Mersey's opinion, vilified Lord and his supposed callous indifference. He was forced to resign from the Leyland Line, for whom he had worked more than fourteen years. The Board of Trade refused to re-open investigation into the matter in 1912 and again in 1913.

Little credence was given to evidence presented during the original Board of Trade hearings: *Californian*'s estimated position, stopped in ice, from seventeen to twenty miles away from the sinking site; the fact that the vessel seen from *Titanic* during the sinking was *moving*; that the nearby lights of yet another ship were seen from *Californian*'s bridge; that several other vessels were in *Titanic*'s vicinity during and immediately after the disaster. . .

With the advent of World War I Captain Lord abandoned efforts to have his case reheard.

Captain of the Californian *in 1912, Stanley Lord in a photograph taken by his son on 13 September 1957, Captain Lord's 80th birthday. (With kind permission of his son, Stanley T. Lord.)*

With the assistance of Frank Strachan, the Leyland Line's American agent, Captain Lord obtained a command in the fleet of the London-based Nitrate Producers Steam Ship Co Ltd (Lawther, Latta & Co). He entered their services in February 1913 and held command until March 1927, including sea service during the war. While still deeply hurt by Mersey's allegations, Lord found that his association with the *Titanic* inquiry did not affect him personally or professionally during this period. He let the matter drop.

After his 1927 retirement Stanley Lord had little awareness of the public's continued interest in *Titanic*. He was not an avid reader. When the 1955 book *A Night to Remember* was serialised in the *Liverpool Daily Echo*, Lord — no relation to the book's author Walter Lord — read parts of it. But the parts he read contained no reference to *Californian* and made little impression on him.

However, with the 1958 release of the film based on *A Night to Remember*, Captain Lord became aware that, in his words, '. . .the film gave great prominence to the allegation that *Californian* stood by in close proximity to the sinking *Titanic*'.

In efforts to clear his name and present publicly the facts not brought out by the British inquiry, Captain Lord enlisted the services of W. Leslie Harrison, general secretary of the British Mercantile Marine Service Association, of which Lord had been a member continuously since 1897. Acting on behalf of *Californian*'s former master, Harrison corresponded with the book's author and the film's producer, requesting that they grant consideration to the captain's side of the story. But both author and producer maintained that the British inquiry findings were authoritative and provided sufficient justification for the references to *Californian* in their respective works.

With the active participation of Captain Lord, who had carefully retained all his original 1912-13 correspondence and personal documents pertaining to the case, Leslie Harrison prepared a petition to the British Board of Trade to re-open the 1912 hearings to correct their findings regarding Lord.

Captain Lord, never in good health since retirement from the sea in 1927, died on 24 January 1962. He was never in any doubt that, even if he had known of *Titanic*'s sinking, he would have been unable to reach the disaster site in time to save any lives. In daylight it had taken from 6 am to 8.30 am to reach the spot where *Carpathia* was taking aboard the last survivors. Lord always maintained that if he had known of the disaster and tried to traverse the extensive ice-field at night, he would have joined *Titanic* on the bottom.

Captain Lord's death did not deter Leslie Harrison from pursuing his own wish — and duty — of trying to clear the captain's name. In February 1965 he presented to the Board of Trade a position paper setting forth the facts as he saw them, some of which were not offered in the 1912 inquiry, and requesting a reversal of the original board's findings.

Not included in the petition was mention of a confidential report made by the first officer of the Norwegian sealing ship *Samson* to Norwegian authorities in April 1912. The report, not made public until 1962, described in some detail how *Samson* purported to have been close enough to the sinking *Titanic* to see the liner's lights and to view the distress rockets being fired.

Samson's master failed to intervene because he feared his own vessel was in violation of territorial seal-hunting regulations and that the rockets represented official attempts at signalling other ships to intercept his own. *Samson* had no wireless, which might have ascertained the situation. After sighting the rockets, the vessel is alleged to have changed course and headed northwards, away from the activity.

Harrison's first petition concluded that the vessels seen by *Titanic* and *Californian* were different ships; that Lord Mersey failed to consider that relative times kept by *Titanic* and *Californian* differed by twelve minutes; that '. . .personal opinions expressed by *Californian*'s third officer and her assistant donkeyman, that the ship they saw must have been *Titanic*, were in fact invalidated by their own evidence and consequently did not justify the extreme importance attached to them by the Court'.

Particularly poignant is Harrison's conclusion that 'The British Court of Inquiry failed in their duty to warn Captain Lord that his position before them was not simply that of a witness; that in consequence he was not given proper opportunity to defend himself; and this failure also deprived him of what otherwise would have been a statutory right of appeal'.

In a letter dated 6 September 1965 the British Board of Trade rejected the petition. In their view, no new and important evidence had been presented. The Board also cited the time which had elapsed since the original hearing, and the deaths of a majority of those involved, including the petitioner.

Marshalling his facts and forces, Leslie Harrison presented yet another petition to the Board of Trade on 4 March 1968. In it, he included new evidence from Lawrence Beesley, a science teacher and author of the book *The Loss of the Titanic*, long accepted as the most reliable factual account of the disaster.

Beesley, a second class *Titanic* passenger, had not been called to testify at either the American or British inquiries. In February 1963 he made a sworn declaration regarding *Titanic*'s distress rockets, but requested that this evidence not be made public until after his death. When this occurred in 1967, Leslie Harrison was able to incorporate the affidavit in his second petition.

Beesley swore that he personally had observed 'about eight distress rockets fired'. He continued, 'I left the ship in No. 13 lifeboat and I am quite confident that the last of these rockets had been fired *before* [Beesley's italics] this lifeboat cleared *Titanic*'s side after being lowered into the water'.

Members of *Californian*'s crew had stated that they observed rockets being fired until 2 am. *Titanic*'s boat number 13 had left the sinking ship at about 1.30 am. Even allowing for the twelve-minute difference in relative ships' times, the discrepancy between the two statements is evident — enough to give cause for a reconsideration of the official stand.

The Board of Trade rejected the second petition on Captain Lord's behalf, saying there had been no miscarriage of justice in the original hearings and that the majority of the people concerned had died. Beesley's evidence was rejected because it was 'not evidence that could not have been produced at the [original] inquiry and also because that evidence is not "important" within the meaning of the Section' of the Merchant Shipping Act of 1894 requiring reopening of a hearing if important new evidence is produced.

And so the matter stands today — awaiting another presentation, a reconsideration, an official recognition of what appears so evident to those who study the *facts*: Captain Stanley Lord not being given the opportunity to explain or defend himself at the original inquiry; allegations being made against him long after he had left the stand as a witness assisting the inquiry; *Californian* being some seventeen to twenty (or even more) miles away from the stricken *Titanic*; the unreliability of the principal witnesses against Lord; the statement of Dr Robert Ballard, who found *Titanic*'s remains in 1985, saying the wreck lies 'to the south and east of the distress position', thus placing *Titanic* and *Californian* even further apart. Perhaps most important of all: the possible presence of two or more other ships closer to *Titanic* than was Lord's vessel.

TEN

Dateline: North Atlantic

Almost before the 'cold waters of the North Atlantic closed over her stern plates', efforts — or at least suggestions — were afoot to salvage *Titanic*. Soon after the disaster a consortium of wealthy families (Guggenheims, Astors and Wideners) contracted with the Merritt and Chapman Derrick and Wrecking Company to raise *Titanic*. Merritt and Chapman studied the proposal but concluded that their 1912 equipment was inadequate to attempt salvage at the great depth involved.

Legends concerning highly valuable cargo, diamonds and gems, vast amounts of gold ingots, large quantities of valuable registered mail, and a fabulous jewelled copy of *The Rubaiyat* were soon well established. Over the years the tales grew until, to many, *Titanic*'s remains represented an immense treasure trove of almost limitless potential.

The truth, though known, was ignored in favour of greed, romantic imagination and media hyperbole. *Titanic*'s cargo manifest had been published on 19 April 1912 in several New York newspapers. The cargo was mundane, typical of the commercial goods most express liners carried during the period. There was no gold listed on the manifest, nor did the company's official cargo stowage diagram show any in the ship's specie room. No insurance claims were filed for valuable diamonds or other gems, apart from a few claims for personal jewellery.

The copy of *The Rubaiyat*, undoubtedly of historic interest, had recently been sold at a 1912 London auction for £405 ($2,025). Assuming present-day monetary values to be ten times (or even one hundred times) the 1912 rates, they would scarcely compensate for the estimated £9 or £10 million required to mount a salvage expedition, plus the many thousands necessary to sustain each day's operations.

Yet through the passing decades, *Titanic*'s retrieval has been the subject of many plans and schemes: compressed air, polyurethane foam, electrolysis of seawater to create hydrogen and oxygen for lift, deep-sea submersibles with remote-controlled 'arms', bags filled with petroleum jelly, encasing the ship in ice formed by liquid nitrogen. . .these schemes and others, it was said, could raise the sunken liner once she was found.

Technical limitations had caused Merritt and Chapman's decision to decline a salvage attempt. Subsequent schemes, too, were limited by inadequate equipment, inexpert knowledge, funding problems or failure to consider basic physical laws. Even the wreck's exact location remained elusive.

During the summer of 1953 the Southampton (UK) salvage firm of Risdon, Beasley

Ltd attempted to locate *Titanic*. Using high explosives to obtain echo profiles, the firm spent seven days in the vicinity of 43.65 N, 52.04 W aboard their salvage vessel *Help*. Their effort was unsuccessful.

Between 1968 and 1978 individuals such as Douglas Woolley, Mark Bamford, Joe King and his partner Spencer Sokale spent countless hours planning expeditions to discover and retrieve *Titanic*'s remains — and working out how to finance the efforts.

In 1977 a group of West Berlin businessmen set up Titanic-Tresor as a backing for Douglas Woolley; in September 1977 they withdrew their support. Also during 1977 a company named Seaonics was formed to investigate the wreck's location and to plan for its exploration. This group involved several prominent scientists and explorers.

During 1978 Walt Disney Productions, in collaboration with *National Geographic* magazine, investigated the possibility of making a full-length film of the disaster. Feasibility studies involving deep under-water photography were conducted by the Alcoa Corporation, owners of the submersible *Aluminaut*. The project was dropped late the same year.

In 1979 the British company Seawise & Titanic Salvage was formed. Headed by Clive Ramsay and Philip Slade — with the expertise of Derek Berwin, under-water photographic expert and Commander John Grattan, under-water diving consultant — the group was funded by industrialist/financier Sir James Goldsmith, who hoped to profit through exclusive coverage for his magazine, *Now*.

This was by far the best thought out group to undertake actual exploration of the wreck. (The others, up to this point, had been involved principally in research.) The original 'base position' established was in the vicinity of 41.40 N, 50.03 W, a site whose co-ordinates were subsequently re-assessed. The expedition was planned for the summer of 1980, but the group failed to obtain sponsorship and was forced to suspend operations.

By this time American scientists on both the west coast (California's Scripps Institute of Oceanography) and the east (Massachusetts' Woods Hole Oceanographic Institution) were showing interest in *Titanic*'s wreck. (The two research organizations would later share a June 1981 exploratory voyage, funded by the United States Office of Naval Research.)

In New York City, Columbia University's Lamont-Doherty Geological Observatory seemingly became the scientific arm of a group headed by Texas oil man Jack Grimm and his partner, Florida film-maker Mike Harris. In earlier undertakings, Grimm had led searches for such historical artefacts as Bigfoot (a sort of colonial 'Abominable Snowman' also known locally as 'Sasquatch'), the Loch Ness monster and Noah's Ark, whose 350-cubit [525-foot] gopher wood hull traditionally rests on top of Turkey's 16,946-foot high Mount Ararat. Grimm's group hoped to realise a profit from *Titanic*'s exploration through the sale of photographs, books and a film.

Their 1980 voyage aboard the research vessel *H. J. W. Fay* carried them to the area of 41.40/41.50 N, 50.00/50.10 W. Hampered by almost continuous bad weather throughout their on-site stay (from 29 July to 17 August), the expedition's members were disappointed in their search. Their sonar soundings produced only some fine, detailed images of the search area's floor.

Competition from Fred Koehler, described by the press as an 'electronics wizard', threatened the exclusivity of Grimm's 1981 expedition. Koehler, of Coral Gables, Florida, sold his electronics repair shop to finance completion of his two-man, 7 by 14½ foot deep-sea submarine, the *Seacopter*. He planned to dive on *Titanic*'s wreck, enter the hull, and remove the legendary diamonds from the purser's safe. Unable to reach agreement with Grimm on *Seacopter*'s use, Koehler set up his own expedition to exploit the wreck. He attracted moderate press attention but no financial backing and his expedition never materialized.

'We have highly technical equipment, and unless we're looking in the wrong area, and I don't believe we are, we'll find her.' With these optimistic words to the press, Grimm left on his 1981 expedition aboard the research vessel *Gyre*. He and his band of intrepid scientists reached their search site three days after the joint Scripps/Woods Hole expedition left the same general area. On station between 9 July and 18 July at approximately 41.39/41.44 N, 50.02/50.08 W, Grimm's second try also was hampered by storms.

There was to be yet another Grimm attempt in 1983, aboard the *Robert D. Conrad*. While Grimm declared that a rounded object first photographed in 1980 was one of *Titanic*'s propeller blades, maritime experts and oceanographers remained convinced it was a rock outcropping.

Beset by technical difficulties, internal management conflicts, incomplete historical research and unco-operative weather, the three expeditions had produced meagre results for their multi-million-dollar costs. Rather than answer questions, they had posed more: was *Titanic*'s 'CQD position' of 41.46 N, 50.14 W — where the expeditions had searched — correct? Had she been buried by a 1929 undersea earthquake? The world's press and *Titanic* scholars speculated. It seemed the ship never would be found.

By 1984, the glare of *Titanic* publicity had subsided. Editors now treated *Titanic* search stories with scepticism and minimal display. In a more productive atmosphere, two respected scientific organizations, the *Institute Français de Recherches pour l'Exploitation des Mers* (the French Institute for Research and Exploitation of the Seas) and the Woods Hole Oceanographic Institution continued quiet preparations for a joint under-water expedition. Jean Jarry of *IFREMER* and Robert D. Ballard of the Woods Hole Oceanographic Institution's Deep Submergence Laboratory headed the mission.

French taxpayers and the prestigious National Geographic Society picked up part of the cost. Officially, the mission was described as 'deep-water engineering tests' of innovative, remoted-controlled under-water equipment, with *Titanic*'s discovery a hoped-for but secondary bonus.

The equipment was, in fact, the first components of an advanced system, called ARGO-Jason, which in final form would permit scientists to photograph and work efficiently in the oceans' depths without leaving their surface vessels. Because of its national security implications, the United States Navy's Office of Naval Research funded ARGO-Jason's development with a $2.8 million (£1.87 million) grant to Woods Hole's Deep Submergence Laboratory in 1983.

On 1 July 1985 the expedition's first phase began as the French left for the disaster site aboard their research vessel *Le Surôit*. Armed with considerable historical research and co-ordinates of the areas unsuccessfully searched in the three Grimm expeditions, the French concentrated their efforts in a 150-square-mile area largely to the south and east of *Titanic*'s distress position. They arrived on 9 July.

The French brought their new side-scanning sonar system, capable of 3,000-feet-wide, highly-detailed sweeps over the ocean floor. Upon their subsequent arrival, the Americans contributed two remote-controlled, sonar-guided camera packages, ARGO and ANGUS, to photograph the liner, once found.

For ten days, *Le Surôit* criss-crossed the designated area in an operation known to the crew as 'mowing the lawn'. No sign of *Titanic* was found. With relentless monotony the vessel towed the side-scan sonar around the clock, as scientists poured over reams of print-outs. Their vigil was interrupted by a 45-knot gale that lasted two full days.

On 19 July the French left for refuelling and supplies at St Pierre et Miquelon, near Newfoundland. Here, Ballard and some of his team joined *Le Surôit* for a second try, resuming on 26 July. By 7 August, the French and their American colleagues had scanned eighty per cent of the search area without success. Time had run out — *Le Surôit* was required elsewhere. Shortly before *Le Surôit* returned home, the Americans and several French colleagues flew to the Azores where they joined the Woods Hole research vessel *Knorr*. On 15 August she left Ponta Delgada with 24 scientists and 25 crew aboard.

Before tackling *Titanic*, a 'warm-up exercise' was necessary. Thus the *Knorr* detoured to the south-east, and on 17 August stopped over remains of the American nuclear submarine *Scorpion*, lost in 1968 with all on board. The ANGUS and ARGO camera systems were deployed, and apparently succeeded in photographing the submarine's wreckage, presumably providing clues about her loss. (The classified pictures have not been released publicly.)

With systems and procedures thoroughly tested, *Knorr* then set out for the *Titanic* search area, arriving there on 22 August. ARGO, containing video cameras and a sonar system, was lowered some 2½ miles down, and round-the-clock searching resumed under watchful chief scientists Ballard and Jean-Louis Michel.

The 'anomalies' once thought by the Grimm expeditions to be parts of *Titanic* were quickly despatched; observation confirmed all, including the so-called 'propeller', to have been large boulders. The expedition then began searching for a debris field, concentrating on the area the French had not surveyed.

Day after day, for about a fortnight, the television screens revealed only the sandy undersea floor. The mission experienced extraordinary weather; the sea was quite flat, as it had been the night *Titanic* sank. The routine was numbing: hour after hour observers sat before the televisions, watching for some sign of *Titanic*'s presence.

Early on the morning of 1 September 1985, Ballard was relaxing in his quarters with a book. Jean-Louis Michel, in the control room, recalled:

'I was on watch at the time of the discovery. . .at 1 am with members of my

On 1 September 1985 the US Navy research vessel Knorr *located the wreck of the* Titanic. *(© 1985 Woods Hole Oceanographic Institution; Reprinted by permission.)*

team. The first indication came from the video where unnatural forms appeared. Our attention was captured by objects lying on the bottom, and within a few minutes more and more of these man-made objects appeared on our screen, until the apparition of a boiler clearly belonging to the *Titanic*.

'[I acted] to prevent the vehicle from hitting any obstacle [below] by raising the altitude of the ARGO, to send somebody to wake Bob [Ballard], Captain Bowen and my French colleagues. . . Within a few minutes the control room was much too crowded. . . My joy was tempered by the fact that I knew we were on the site of a tragedy; I shared this moment with my 40-man team of *Le Suroît*, who should have been there.'

The ship's cook roused Ballard, who confirmed that the boiler was *Titanic*'s. Some three-dozen had jammed the control room, and someone remarked that it was 1.40 am. Remembering that *Titanic* had sunk at 2.20, Ballard led everyone to the ship's stern, where they observed a brief silence for those lost in the disaster.

Since the site's geography was unknown, the expedition was greatly concerned about accidentally striking the wreck with the camera package. Ballard gave orders to haul ARGO up until fathometer and sonar readings could pin-point the area's arrangement. A near-catastrophe occurred as the ship's winch broke while hauling ARGO aboard. It took fourteen hours of jury-rigging a spare part before another look at *Titanic* could be obtained.

Meanwhile the expedition deployed a network of under-water transponders which, with the ship's equipment, gave instantaneous accurate information about the relative positions of *Titanic*, *Knorr* and ARGO.

The weather began to deteriorate, and winds built to more than forty knots, with fourteen-foot waves, yet her unique cycloidal propellers enabled *Knorr* to maintain position; underwater photography continued.

It was an exceptionally difficult task: the camera package trailed some 2½ miles downwards from aft of the *Knorr*, pitching in the heavy seas. Ballard and Michel surveyed around the ship, then 'flew' *ARGO* over her. *Titanic* was sitting upright, and initially it appeared that her second and third funnels were still standing. The forward mast had fallen back against the superstructure's port side, but the bow was in remarkably good condition, covered only by light sediment. In a joyous announcement to shore, Ballard said the ship was in 'museum like' condition. Expedition scientists then decided to approach from the stern, but it could not be found. What had become of it? Ballard could only speculate that somehow it had broken off.

The high-'altitude' black-and-white video images from ARGO were an excellent beginning. But with one day remaining before *Knorr* had to return home, it was essential to obtain some close-up photographs of *Titanic*. ANGUS was thus deployed. At times gliding to within a dozen yards of the ship, it recorded a series of stunning views, eerily tinted in blue.

The world soon saw them. The giant hole where number one funnel had been. The anchor chains, frozen in position. The crow's nest and its telephone alcove, now hanging precariously over a forward hatch. Unbroken wine bottles, still corked, but probably now filled with seawater. Debris once part of the ship's structure. The starboard bridge wing, smashed flat by the falling forward funnel (was this how Captain Smith had died?). A piece of shell plating, torn from the hull. Cargo cranes, twisted in the wracking forces during and after the sinking.

ANGUS had to be 'flown blind', with no immediate video feed-back to those controlling it. Ballard called searching near the wreck, 'one of the most harrowing experiences of my life'. It was his concern for *Titanic*'s sanctity — and the multi-million dollar camera unit's welfare — that prompted the decision to attempt only high-altitude, downward-looking views.

There was time for no more. Transponders were retrieved, all equipment was stowed. The voyage home began, but not before an intruding aeroplane had repeatedly circled the ship. The expedition had tried to keep *Titanic*'s exact location a secret to prevent plunderers and armchair salvage experts from disturbing the wreck, possibly damaging it further. With the plane's arrival, it appeared the secret would eventually leak out; *Titanic*'s depth, public opinion, and individual conscience apparently would be all the protection she would have.

As *Knorr* sailed westwards scientists reviewed the mission's data and photographs. The stern — now in pieces — had been located after all, 2,000 feet behind the 'bow section' in the midst of a mile-long debris field.

Thousands of well-wishers, hundreds of reporters and more than a dozen film crews from around the world greeted the expedition at Woods Hole, Massachusetts, on 9 September. The quiet New England town was mobbed by those seeking to learn more about 'the people who found the *Titanic*'. Elsewhere, *Titanic* survivors were being bombarded with interview requests. Once again the White Star ship and her people were headline news.

At a Washington, DC press conference, Ballard concluded his prepared statement saying:

'The *Titanic* itself lies in 13,000 feet of water on a gently sloping alpine-like countryside overlooking a small canyon below.

'Its bow faces north and the ship sits upright on the bottom. Its mighty stacks point upward.

'There is no light at this great depth and little light can be found.

'It is quiet and peaceful and a fitting place for the remains of this greatest of sea tragedies to rest.

'May it forever remain that way and may God bless these found souls.'

His noble idea did not last very long. Within two weeks of the discovery, a Welshman had proposed raising the ship (notwithstanding its fracture into at least two pieces). A British insurance company said it might own the wreck. Several new improbable schemes involving refloating or salvage were announced.

One proposed to raise the ship using giant under-water slings lowered from a 'semi-submersible platform [that] would rest on two water-tight supertankers' (presumably drained of oil). The procedure, admitted promoters, would have to be performed twice, since *Titanic*'s stern had broken off. 'It could take more than five years to complete the salvage operation,' noted a breathless magazine reporter.

'It's like the Great Wall of China,' said a proponent. 'Given enough time and money and people, you can do anything.'

A Belgian entrepreneur promised forty lucky passengers the opportunity to dive in a chartered submarine to the *Titanic*, recover artefacts, then return to the surface for a memorial service marking the sinking's anniversary and featuring several Hollywood celebrities — all for $25,000 (£17,241) apiece.

In an effort to protect the ship, North Carolina Congressman Walter B. Jones introduced the 'Titanic Maritime Memorial Act' in the United States House of Representatives. It called for establishment of strict scientific guidelines for the wreck's exploration and salvage, and asked the American Secretary of State to enter into discussions with Canada, the United Kingdom and France, urging them to pass similar legislation. By late 1986 the bill had overwhelmingly passed the House and Senate. On 21 October 1986 President

Ronald Reagan signed the measure into law. It might well be a moot gesture: *Titanic* lies in international waters beyond any legal jurisdiction, some law experts said.

Two Englishmen felt otherwise. On 5 November 1985, just two months after *Titanic's* discovery, Leslie Pink and Leonard Brown founded the Titanic Preservation Trust in Portsmouth. Declaring that 'delving in the innards of the *Titanic*, two-and-a-half miles down in the Atlantic, is like trespassing with intent to do damage in a graveyard,' the Trust hoped to 'encourage litigation to keep the ship and its contents together as a memorial, instead of fragments and contents being removed piecemeal to go to various bidders'. The group would support 'restrained archaeological and oceanographic research at the site of the foundered vessel'.

While answering some questions, an expedition had once again posed new ones. When and why had the ship broken up? In how many pieces had she broken? How large was the iceberg's gash, and where was it located? Was the ship really in 'museum-like' condition? The overhead views of *Titanic* provided mere hints about the night of 14-15 April. It was apparent that there was still more to learn. And apparent, too, was the need for a manned craft that could negotiate safely around *Titanic's* broken hull to take pictures from additional angles and viewpoints.

Once again, under-water equipment tests provided the basis for another visit to the ship. Jason Jr (or 'JJ'), a prototype of the Jason portion of Woods Hole's undersea exploration system, was ready for trials, funded by a $220,000 (£146,700) US Navy grant.

Jason Jr was a lawnmower-sized, self-propelled, high-tech camera unit, powered and

For the 1986 expedition, the Woods Hole team used the research vessel Atlantis II, *seen here launching the deep-diving submersible* Alvin *over the* Titanic's *final resting place. (© 1986 Woods Hole Oceanographic Institution; Reprinted by permission.)*

controlled through a 250-foot-long umbilical cord. Its four thrusters allowed instantaneous manoeuvring even in tight quarters in depths up to 20,000 feet. It carried high-resolution colour video and still cameras and powerful light sources. JJ's use would pinpoint modifications needed on Jason itself, the larger, more capable unit planned for 1989. Navy personnel joined the 1986 expedition for hands-on operating experience. Once again, Dr Robert Ballard headed the team.

Ultimately, Jason would be launched from ARGO. But its predecessor Jason Jr required a ride to the ocean floor. The three-man deep-diving submersible *Alvin*, a veteran of more than 1,700 dives since its construction in 1964, was specially modified to increase its depth capabilities and to accept the hitch-hiking JJ, mounted in a basket-like 'garage' on *Alvin*'s forward end.

The Woods Hole research vessel *Atlantis II* sailed for the *Titanic* site on 9 July 1986, carrying 56 scientists and crew. Not on board were *IFREMER*'s representatives, who had had disagreements with the Americans over the release of photographs from the 1985 expedition.

A 3½-day voyage brought *Atlantis II* to the wreck site without difficulty. The sunken liner's exact co-ordinates, kept in a safe, had been fed into *Atlantis II*'s navigational computer, taking her directly to the spot.

The expedition first installed a series of transponders near *Titanic*'s location, allowing pin-point positioning to within tens of metres, vitally important for *Alvin*'s safety.

Alvin's first dive, number 1705 of her busy career, began on Sunday 13 July. Dr Ballard and two crewmen played classical music on one of *Alvin*'s tape recorders during their 2½-hour descent to the ship's final resting place, some 13,000 feet below.

As pressure on *Alvin*'s titanium hull mounted steadily, water temperature dropped. Sunlight quickly faded to gloom, and then to perpetual blackness. Ballard noticed rivulets of water forming on the submersible's inside walls. Outside pressure was now 6,500 pounds per square inch and he expressed concern to the two *Alvin* crewmen. They reassured him such water condensation was normal.

The downward journey ended. With guidance from *Atlantis II*, the submarine inched forward on its electric motors, its powerful electric lights piercing the abyssal darkness. Suddenly, the search was over. Before them lay 'a tremendous black wall of steel [that] seemed endless in all directions,' as Ballard described it. For the first time in 74 years, human beings were seeing *Titanic* first hand.

The reverie was brought to an abrupt end after just a few minutes. Alarm bells clamorously announced that, somehow, sea water was reaching *Alvin*'s batteries, upon which everything — including vital life support systems — depended. There was no more time for *Titanic* observations. It was necessary to get to the surface, and quickly. Chief pilot Ralph Hollis released ballast, manoeuvring slightly to ensure it would not fall on to *Titanic*, and the submarine rapidly ascended.

Safely on board *Atlantis II*, *Alvin* was put in technicians' care. Repair time would not be wasted. ANGUS, a 1985 expedition veteran, was towed over the wreck in a nightly

Above *Rust covers two bollards located forward on the starboard side of the sunken vessel. (© 1986 Woods Hole Oceanographic Institution; Reprinted by permission.)*

Below *An unbroken window marks a first class single berth cabin on* Titanic's *starboard boat deck, aft of the officers' quarters. (© 1986 Woods Hole Oceanographic Institution; Reprinted by permission.)*

Above *An electric lifeboat winch on the starboard side of the boat deck lies under a heavy mantle of corrosion. (© 1986 Woods Hole Oceanographic Institution; Reprinted by permission.)*

Below *The camera aboard ANGUS, the unmanned towed vehicle, peers directly into the collapsed remains of* Titanic's *forward first class entrance. To the left of the hole is the roof over elevator machinery. (© 1986 Woods Hole Oceanographic Institution; Reprinted by permission.)*

Above *The portside aft corner of the ventilation shaft at the base of the second funnel (top) has had its louvred grating torn away. The large circular hole marks the former location of a cowl ventilator above the first class reading room. To the right the decking begins its steep downward plunge aft to the breaking point. (© 1986 Woods Hole Oceanographic Institution; Reprinted by permission.)*

Below *The unbroken, inch-thick glass of a midships porthole resists the rivers of rust cascading down the vessel's side. (© 1986 Woods Hole Oceanographic Institution; Reprinted by permission.)*

Above *The 1986 expedition located the 200-foot stern section, lying almost 2,000 feet from the bow and rotated 180 degrees from the bow section. A cargo crane juts out over the starboard side; the cowling for the crane's heavy duty electric motors has been torn away, revealing white porcelain electric insulators. (© 1986 Woods Hole Oceanographic Institution; Reprinted by permission.)*

Below *The chaotic appearance of* Titanic's *stern section reflects the immense forces that wracked the area upon its impact with the sea bed. Electrical cables, torn from their conduits, criss-cross the underside of a deck bent backwards over the rest of the stern (right). (© 1986 Woods Hole Oceanographic Institution; Reprinted by permission.)*

ritual providing photographic and video reconnaissance for the following day's manned search. Meanwhile, other technicians tested Jason Jr and connected it for the first time to *Alvin.*

Launch procedures were established quickly. Each morning, *Alvin* would be deposited on the ocean's surface with JJ in its 'garage'. After a five-minute check-out, the submarine would then descend in a free-fall to the *Titanic.* The deposit point was 'upstream' of *Titanic*'s position, with moderately strong undersea currents pushing the submarine closer to the ship. Eventually, the expedition could place *Alvin* in such a way as to arrive within 150 feet of *Titanic* after a 13,000 foot descent.

Working conditions inside *Alvin* were cramped and uncomfortable. Her pilot sat or kneeled at the front porthole. To the portside was JJ's operator, while the dive's scientist was at the starboard viewing port. Ballard said the experience was 'like working inside a Swiss watch'.

Dive number two examined the forward first class entrance's collapsed dome, through which Ballard planned to send JJ on the next dive. The dive provided four hours for photographing the ship and ascertaining its condition and arrangement.

'We couldn't see the [*Titanic*'s] name,' Ballard radioed *Atlantis II*. 'There are rivers of rust pouring down the side of the ship and running down into the sediment.' Presumably, the indented, eighteen-inch high, gold-painted letters were well hidden by corrosion.

Alvin then headed for the wheelhouse. 'We landed where the wheelhouse was and saw the ship's wheel minus the wood,' he reported. The wheelhouse itself, also made of wood, had been eaten down to a six-inch-high nub. Ballard reported that all wood had been consumed by undersea worms whose calcified skeletons now cover much of the ship. The submarine then headed for the opening for number one funnel, moving aft and out over the collapsed grand staircase dome.

Dive number three was to feature JJ's debut. Upon arrival at the wreck, the explorers found strong ocean currents that hadn't been there before. Sweeping across *Titanic* from the starboard side aft to the port side forward, they repeatedly forced *Alvin* toward the *Titanic*'s towering hull. With the strong current rendering JJ's deployment impossible, Ballard and the crew used the time to photograph the ship more fully, including her previously-unseen port side.

The dive concluded, Ballard radioed its findings to shore. 'Today was a hard dive,' he said. 'The current was very strong and there was a lot of ticklish matter in the water, so it was a hard-working dive. . . The objective today was still imagery. We saw the beautiful light on the [top of the forward] mast, a big brass fixture, and we could see a lot of door knobs [and] things like that.'

Next morning the current had quietened considerably. *Alvin* 'landed' next to the gaping hole that was once *Titanic*'s forward grand staircase. Using controls resembling those of a video game, JJ's pilot Martin Bowen gingerly nudged the robot out of its 'garage' and into the ship. As one newspaper headline put it, 'After 74 years, *Titanic* has guests'.

Downwards the 'swimming eyeball' went, perhaps reaching as far as B deck. The ship's interior was an utter shambles. Only the steel columns that had supported the dome and staircase survived. All wood had disappeared here, too. The staircase's lower portion was filled with debris. Several crystal-and-brass light fixtures still hung from their overhead wires, accompanied by an unending succession of yellow, red, brown and orange stalactites.

On 16 July dive number five commenced. A landing near the bridge included a close-up examination of the metallic remnants of the ship's wheel. A tense moment arose when JJ's control cable became badly snagged on a piece of jagged metal. Bowen's repeated back-and-forth manoeuvring eventually freed the craft without damage.

An attempt to go through 'A' deck's large windows for another inside look was blocked; JJ was a bit too big to fit. 'He'll have to go on a diet,' Ballard quipped. The expedition instead peered through some of the many unbroken first class cabin portholes. Like the public rooms, *Titanic*'s staterooms are filled only with dangling rust deposits and debris. Coming up along the ship's side, the submarine bumped an overhanging lifeboat davit, sending a shower of rust fluttering down.

JJ was then sent to inspect the crow's nest and the foremast's navigation light. The submersible next moved aft along the boat deck, and again 'parked' near the grand staircase for a brief interior look.

'I'm very relieved not to find any human remains,' Dr Ballard reported at the conclusion of the dive. The sea and its creatures appear to have claimed *Titanic*'s people. Scientists said the water's low mineral content and steady bottom currents aided the dissolving process.

Exploration continued. The 18 July dive concentrated on the debris field near the ship's stern. Ballard reported sighting 'thousands and thousands of items laid all over the bottom,' the vast majority from second or third class areas of the ship. They included chamber pots, electric stateroom heaters, dishes, cups, pots and pans from the galley, thousands of lumps of coal, and several of the ship's four safes, emptied during the ship's evacuation, according to eye-witness reports.

Approaching the largest, probably from the second class purser's office, *Alvin*'s manipulator arm gave the handle a tug, but the Milner's safe remained secure. 'It had a big handle of bronze or gold, and we saw the dial.' The door bore a 'beautiful crest,' and was 'polished and clean; it looked brand new,' Ballard said.

Only a handful of personal belongings were found. They included a shoe, the porcelain head of a child's doll, and a Romanesque statue.

After six ten-hour dives in six days, crew fatigue caused 19 July to be a day of rest. Technicians swarmed over *Alvin* and JJ, doing necessary maintenance. Meanwhile, scientists examined photographs to plan future dives.

The seventh dive was a departure from previous ones: Ballard remained on *Atlantis II*, and three Navy personnel dived to *Titanic* to gain valuable experience in operating Jason Jr and *Alvin*.

Working some 2,000 feet behind the bow section, dive eight concentrated on the mangled and broken stern section. It was a sobering visit that left the explorers deeply moved with the realisation that hundreds of *Titanic*'s people had spent their last few terrifying moments

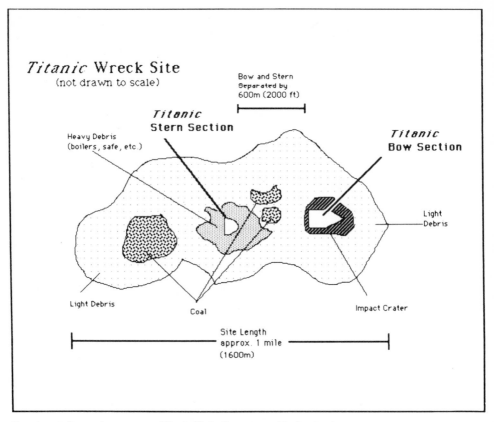

Based on information courtesy Woods Hole Oceanographic Institution.

here. 'It was the hardest place to work emotionally,' Ballard recalled.

Explorers were surprised to find a large stern section in basically one piece, sitting upright and pointing in the same direction as the bow. While the rudder's upper portions could be discerned, the ship's propellers were deeply buried in sediment or debris. Other stern pieces were damaged almost beyond recognition. Ballard called the stern 'a carnage of debris. It looked violent and torn, fragmented and jumbled like a rat's nest'.

The poop deck was peeled up and flattened back on itself, exposing under-deck beams and electrical cables. A 2½-ton cargo crane was twisted outwards over the ship's side. The stern's unpredictable shapes made diving difficult and dangerous.

Apparently, *Titanic*'s hull had broken on or near the surface. The huge engines plummeted quickly to the ocean floor, while bow and stern sections pirouetted to points some distance away. As they spiralled downwards, their contents scattered, forming the debris field.

On one occasion, JJ provided some moments of high drama. As *Alvin* surfaced in heavy seas, the robot fell out of its 'garage' and dangled from its umbilical cable which chafed against a cutting tool on the submarine's bow. With each passing swell, damage became increasingly likely, and only prompt action prevented the cable's severing and loss of the multi-million-dollar robot. Later, two days of dives had to be cancelled because of other electrical problems with JJ.

A historical accident also occurred. As ANGUS was hauled aboard after a night of unmanned photography, it was found to have snagged a steel cable from *Titanic*. Throughout the mission, personnel had adhered scrupulously to a 'hands off' policy regarding *Titanic* artefacts. As Ballard later put it, 'We thought the artefacts looked better exactly where they were'. Reverence and respect were observed. The wayward cable was dropped overboard immediately, and crewmen executing the order were asked to wash their hands, lest *Titanic* rust remain behind.

Another dive examined the break between the second and third funnels. At the bow section's after end, the decks had collapsed together as though crushed from the top, pulling the ship's hull plating inwards. The decks lie flat, suggesting the rupture was more of a direct pull than a twisting motion.

The expedition attempted to ascertain the iceberg's damage. But *Titanic*'s bow section had struck the bottom at a 45-degree angle, ploughing up the bottom for perhaps a hundred feet. When it came to a stop, the bow was buried fifty feet deep in debris with the ship's anchors, still in place, just a few feet above the ocean floor. Thus the iceberg's gash could not be inspected. 'I'm glad the bow and stern are buried so deeply,' Ballard said later, for this factor would make salvaging unfeasible. 'The *Titanic* will protect itself. It's very fragile and any attempt to raise it would break it up.'

Buckled plates and sprung seams were found below the superstructure's forward end. Ballard suggested these may have been iceberg-related, but subsequent evaluation indicates that impact with the bottom probably caused them.

It was impossible to obtain views of the wreck as a whole — *Titanic* simply was too large. Ballard likened the experience to 'walking in a redwood forest at night with only a flashlight. You can take great pictures of the bark, but not of the tree'. The extensive photographing of individual pieces eventually would allow construction of a 'photo-mosaic' of the entire site.

Alvin's 1,715th career dive was her last to *Titanic*. JJ managed to find its way on to the promenade deck and discovered a brass plaque marking a stairway for crew only. As a final activity, a plaque was placed on *Titanic*'s bow, asking all who might come later to respect the ship as a memorial site.

The mission was over. In eleven journeys to the great liner and through nightly unmanned examination, more than 50,000 still pictures and 100 hours of video-tape footage were obtained. Scientists and support personnel felt a tired jubilation at the successes of their 'picture-perfect cruise'. After retrieving the transponders, *Atlantis II* sailed for home.

The explorers were greeted by 500 friends, relatives, reporters and Woods Hole colleagues upon their 28 July arrival. Within a week, Texas oil man Jack Grimm had announced his intentions to retrieve artefacts from the ship. 'I can't see them just lie there and be absorbed by the ocean floor,' he pronounced. '. . . What possible harm can [artefact salvage] do to this mass of twisted steel?' He entered into negotiations with *IFREMER* to mount a 1987 expedition to *Titanic*, with joint ownership of anything retrieved.

Ironically, the same technology that had brought the world its first glimpses of the lost liner, the superior science that had awed the world through respectful, gentle exploration could now expose the ship to potentially its greatest danger since 14-15 April 1912.

Perhaps before scientists and historians can learn the lessons to be found in the site's arrangement and contents, perhaps before two-dozen living *Titanic* survivors are beyond the pain that salvage activities surely would bring, and perhaps despite the principles espoused in the *Titanic* Maritime Memorial Act, the symbolic final resting place of 1,523 men, women and children will be disturbed and forever altered.

In 1985, the scientist who had found *Titanic* likened her to an archaeological site. 'The great pyramids of the deep are now accessible to man. He can either plunder them like the grave robbers of Egypt or protect them for the countless generations which will follow ours,' Robert Ballard said.

Time had played such a pivotal role in *Titanic*'s one disastrous voyage. Now, after 75 years of peaceful solitude, time will determine the quality and length of her future. . .

Appendix One

To help judge *Titanic*'s dimensions and capacities, the following comparisons may be made between the White Star ship, *Mauretania* (potentially her chief rival of the period) and the *United States*, the most technically successful Atlantic Liner.

	Titanic	Mauretania	United States
Laid down	31 March 1909	September 1904	8 February 1950
Launched	31 May 1911	20 September 1906	23 June 1951
Maiden voyage	10 April 1912	16 November 1907	3 July 1952
Length (overall)	882ft 9in	785ft	990ft
Beam	92ft 6in	88ft	102ft
Moulded depth	59ft 6in	57ft	72ft
Tonnage: gross	46,329	31,938	50,924
net	21,831	8,948	24,475
Decks	7	7	7
Engines	2 triple expansion and 1 turbine	4 turbines	4 turbines
Total horsepower	46,000	68,000	240,000
Service speed	21 knots	25 knots	33 knots
Top speed (est)	23-24 knots	'over 30 knots'	'over 38 knots'
Passengers—1st class	735	563	882
2nd class	674	464	685
3rd class	1,026	1,138	718
Officers and crew	885	812	1,068
Last voyage	10 April 1912	26 September 1934	1 November 1969
Length of service	4½ days	27 years	17 years

Appendix Two

Titanic's brief life can be measured in hours. The following are some significant dates and times in this short period:

1909

31 March		Keel laid (hull number 390904).

1911

31 May		Launched.

1912

20 March		Original scheduled date for maiden voyage departure; postponed due to construction delays caused by repairs to *Olympic* at Belfast following collision with HMS *Hawke*.
31 March		Outfitting completed (official number 131428).
1 April		Sea trials, scheduled for this date, postponed due to high winds.
2 April	6 am	Commencement of sea trials in Belfast Lough and the Irish Sea (to 6 pm).
	8 pm	Departs Belfast for Southampton, England. Fire in coal bunker number six.
4 April		Arrives at Southampton shortly after midnight.
10 April	12.15 pm	Departs White Star Dock, Southampton on maiden voyage. Aboard: first class 195; second class 234; third class 497; crew 909; local passengers for Cherbourg and Queenstown 29. Fire burning in coal bunker number six.
	6.35 pm	Arrives Cherbourg, France. Debarks 22 cross-Channel passengers. Takes aboard first class 142; second class 30; third class 102.
	8.10 pm	Departs Cherbourg for Queenstown (Cobh) Ireland.
11 April	11.30 am	Arrives Queenstown. Debarks seven local passengers. One crewman deserts. Takes aboard second class 7; third class 113. Total aboard 1,320 passengers, 908 crew.
	1.30 pm	Departs Queenstown.
		Noon Thursday (11 April) to noon Friday (12 April) 386 miles logged.
12 April		Noon Friday (12 April) to noon Saturday (13 April) 519 miles logged.
13 April		Noon Saturday (13 April) to noon Sunday (14 April) 546 miles logged.
	1 pm	Chief engineer reports fire in coal bunker number six extinguished.

14 April	9 am	*Caronia* reports ice at 42° N, extending from Long 49° to 50°.
	1.42 pm	Ship's position 42°35′ N, 45°50′ W.
		Baltic reports ice 41°50′ N, 49°52′ W.
	1.45 pm	*Amerika* reports ice 41°27′ N, 50°8′ W.
	5.50 pm	Reaches 'The Corner' — 42° N, 47° W. Course changed from S 62° W to S 86° W.
	7 pm	Air temperature 43°.
	7.15 pm	First officer Murdoch orders lamp trimmer Hemming to secure forward fo'c's'le hatch to prevent glow from interfering with the crow's nest watch. Ice warning received at 1.42 pm from *Baltic* posted on bridge.
	7.30 pm	Air temperature 39°.
		Californian reports ice 42°3′ N, 49°9′ W.
	8.40 pm	Officer of the watch Lightoller orders ship's carpenter Maxwell to watch the fresh water supply as it may freeze.
	9 pm	Air temperature 33°.
	9.40 pm	*Mesaba* warns of ice 42° N to 41°25′ N, 49° W to 50°30′ W. Warning not delivered to bridge.
	10 pm	First officer Murdoch relieves second officer Lightoller on the bridge. Look-outs Lee and Fleet relieve Jewell and Symons in crow's nest. Air temperature 32°.
	10.30 pm	Sea temperature 32°. *Rappahannock* passes, reports via morse lamp having just run through heavy ice.
	11 pm	*Californian* tries to warn of ice but is cut off by *Titanic*'s wireless operator.
	11.40 pm	Collision with iceberg.
15 April	midnight	Hogg and Evans relieve Lee and Fleet in crow's nest.
	12.05 am	Captain Smith orders lifeboats uncovered and crew mustered.
	12.10 am	Fourth officer Boxhall works out his estimate of ship's position: 41°46′ N, 50°14′ W.
	12.15 am	First wireless transmission of *Titanic*'s call for assistance — CQD.
	12.45 am	First distress rocket fired. First lifeboat, number 7, lowered. Wireless CQD transmission changed to SOS.
	1.40 am	Last rocket fired.
	2.05 am	Last lifeboat, Collapsible D, lowered.
	2.10 am	Last wireless signal transmitted.
	2.18 am	Lights fail.
	2.20 am	Ship founders, 1,523 lost.
	3.30 am	Rescue ship *Carpathia*'s rockets sighted by drifting lifeboats.
	4.10 am	First lifeboat, number 2, picked up by *Carpathia*.
	8.10 am	Last lifeboat, number 12, picked up.
	8.50 am	*Carpathia* heads for New York with 705 *Titanic* survivors.
18 April	9.25 pm	*Carpathia* docks at Pier 54, North River, New York with *Titanic*'s survivors.

The preceding is only the barest outline of the events in *Titanic*'s life. Times are approximate and are expressed in local (ship's or city's) actual time.

Appendix Three

The courage and bravery of *Titanic*'s crew and passengers is not forgotten. Memorial statues, plaques and buildings are an ever-present reminder of the men and women who stood fast, of those who stood back. The International Ice Patrol, 24-hour manned wireless and sufficient lifeboat accommodation for all passengers now attest to the *Titanic*'s memory.

As long as men sail the seas, as long as the heart swells at hearing 'Nearer, My God, to Thee', the memory of the proud and beautiful *Titanic* and of her heroic crew and courageous passengers will not vanish from the hearts of men and women everywhere.

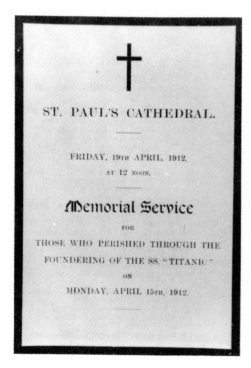

Left *Among the earliest of* Titanic *memorial services was the one at St Paul's Cathedral, London. Shown is the front page of the programme. (Bob Forrest Collection.)*

ST. PAUL'S CATHEDRAL.

FRIDAY, 19TH APRIL, 1912,
AT 12 NOON.

Memorial Service

FOR

THOSE WHO PERISHED THROUGH THE
FOUNDERING OF THE SS. "TITANIC"
ON
MONDAY, APRIL 15TH, 1912.

Right *Bandmaster Wallace Hartley's funeral in his home town of Colne, Lancashire, attracted wide newspaper coverage. (*Daily Sketch.*)*

DAILY SKETCH.

No. 907 —MONDAY, MAY 20, 1912.   THE PREMIER PICTURE PAPER.   (Registered as a Newspaper)   ONE HALFPENNY.

30,000 MOURNERS AT BURIAL OF TITANIC BANDMASTER.

In keeping with the heroism of the man who led the Titanic's band as they stood on the deck of the doomed liner calmly playing "Nearer, my God, to Thee" while the last of the lifeboats pulled away from the sinking ship were the striking scenes witnessed on Saturday when the remains of Mr. Wallace Hartley were laid to rest in the cemetery of his native town of Colne, Lancashire. From all parts of the country, and especially from Lancashire and Yorkshire, flocked crowds, estimated at 30,000, to pay their last tribute of respect to the memory of the central figure of one of the most touching incidents in the history of the sea.

(1) A close friend (X) of the deceased musician at the graveside. (2) Mr. Hartley's father (on right) and the principal mourners. (3) Mr. Hartley (X) and the chief mourners approaching the grave. (4 and 5) The Bethel Choir and the Colne Orchestral Society, who sang the hymn "Nearer, my God, to Thee" as the body was being interred. (6) Leaving the Bethel Chapel, where Mr. Hartley was originally a choirmaster and his father was choirmaster for twenty-five years. Inset: The heroic bandmaster. - *Daily Sketch Photographs.*

Right *Another tribute to* Titanic's *engineers graced a plot of city-donated land adjacent to the Liverpool Landing Stage. (Authors' collection.)*

Far left *Hartley's fellow townspeople erected this memorial to the memory of* Titanic's *brave bandmaster. (Arnold Watson Collection.)*

Left *The 'below decks' memorial was relocated to Southampton's Holy Rood Church in 1972. (Authors' collection.)*

Left *The engineers' memorial in Southampton's public gardens was dedicated in 1914. (Authors' collection.)*

Right *The* Titanic *is remembered in the city of her birth. This memorial stands near Belfast City Hall. (Authors' collection.)*

Above left *The* Titanic *Memorial Lighthouse was a feature of the Seaman's Church Institute building at 25 South Street, New York. When the building was demolished in the 1960's, the lighthouse was moved to the South Street Seaport. (Authors' collection.)*

Above *Helen Melville Smith dedicated this life-sized bronze statue of her gallant father, Captain Edward J. Smith, at Lichfield, Staffordshire. (Arnold Watson Collection.)*

Left *A stone tablet commemorates the heroism of chief wireless operator John George Phillips, as part of the memorial cloister in his home town of Godalming, Surrey. (Marconi Marine.)*

Above *A reclining woman forms the central figure of a fountain dedicated to Isidor and Ida Straus. The memorial is located at Broadway and West 106th Street, New York. (Authors' collection.)*

Below *Mrs William Howard Taft, wife of the late American President, presided at the 1931 dedication of the Women's Titanic Memorial in Washington, DC. (Authors' collection.)*

Index